Unlocking Your Entrepreneurial Potential

Nov., 2011

Don & Pat,

Thanks for your support and "editing" help while I was writing this book. It helped a lot! Hope you enjoy the finished product.

Tim

TIM S. MCENENY

Unlocking Your Entrepreneurial Potential

Marketing, Money, and Management
Strategies for the Self-Funded Entrepreneur

iUniverse, Inc.
Bloomington

Unlocking Your Entrepreneurial Potential
Marketing, Money, and Management Strategies for the Self-Funded Entrepreneur

iUniverse books may be ordered through booksellers or by contacting:

iUniverse
1663 Liberty Drive
Bloomington, IN 47403
www.iuniverse.com
1-800-Authors (1-800-288-4677)

ISBN: 978-1-4620-3244-0 (sc)
ISBN: 978-1-4620-3245-7 (hc)
ISBN: 978-1-4620-3246-4 (e)

Library of Congress Control Number: 2011912852

Printed in the United States of America

iUniverse rev. date: 8/23/2011

Disclaimer

For Laurene, Erika, Tim Jr., Eileen, and Tim III

CONTENTS

FOREWORD

Entrepreneurship is lonely.

No matter how powerful your dream of creating a business, the hard truth is that the dream is usually yours alone. Government offers limited help. Banks run away from the risk. As much as our society celebrates the successful entrepreneur, we do little to help the newborn business get on its feet, much less survive. And the prognosis for that new business usually is not good.

The Small Business Administration will tell you that half of all start-ups fail within just five years. To be sure, in our "survival of the fittest" economy, many start-ups *should* fail. The math simply doesn't work. But even the best ideas often go begging for financial backing. The typical entrepreneur has maxed out his or her credit cards and raided his or her life savings to invest in the dream. In my dozen years of covering the business beat for CBS News, every entrepreneur I've ever encountered (including the most successful) has shared tales of gut-wrenching moments when the cash ran dry and the business teetered on the precipice.

If you're reading this book, you probably know already how hard it is to find investors out there. The reality is, most new entrepreneurs get start-up money by tapping their own bank accounts, their 401(k) plans, and their parents or friends. There is no central clearinghouse for generous angel investors. In fact, there aren't many of those angels out there. And banks don't generally finance start-ups. As Tim points out, 99 percent of new businesses never receive third-party funding.

Despite their high failure rate, new businesses are absolutely critical to our economy. Historically, during the last seven recessions, it's been entrepreneurs who essentially restarted the economy. But this time the damage is far more severe.

The Federal Reserve of Cleveland recently concluded that "the Great Recession was actually a time of considerable decline in entrepreneurial activity in the United States." Crunching numbers from the Bureau of Labor Statistics, the Cleveland Fed found that the US economy lost 146,000 employer businesses between 2007 and 2009. That's especially alarming because employer firms account for 97 percent of private-sector GDP.

While some of the decline was due to the closure of existing businesses, "the largest effect came from a decline in new business formation, particularly for businesses with employees." If the economy is to recover or replace the more than 8 million jobs wiped out in the Great Recession of 2008–2010, we must do everything we can to encourage and rekindle America's entrepreneurial spirit.

How important is entrepreneurship? A 2010 study by the Kauffman Foundation has some striking numbers. It concluded that net job growth in the US economy occurs only through start-up firms. The study revealed that both on average and for all but seven years between 1977 and 2005, "existing firms are net job destroyers, losing one million jobs net combined per year. By contrast, in their first year new firms add an average of 3 million jobs." In other words, it's entrepreneurs who, through their energy and ideas, constantly reinvigorate and grow our economy. We need them. We need you.

That's why Tim McEneny's new book is such a valuable tool. Tim has travelled this route himself. He knows the way. *Unlocking Your Entrepreneurial Potential* will not remove all the obstacles in your path, but it will help you navigate around them. As you enter the tangled forest of entrepreneurship, Tim has provided the road map and a flashlight. Good luck on the journey! With Tim's book as a guide, you are not alone.

Anthony Mason
CBS News, Senior Business Correspondent
New York, New York

Preface

Starting and running your own business can be a very rewarding experience. It provides a great sense of accomplishment and can generate wealth beyond your wildest dreams.

You'll never get rich working for someone else. In fact, almost half the people considered "super rich" say they created their fortunes by owning their own businesses. The best way for the average person to build wealth and gain independence is by starting a business.

Unlocking Your Entrepreneurial Potential is written for people without easy access to capital or high-powered connections. In fact, well over 99 percent of the 6 million new business started every year will *never* receive third-party funding. According to Niels Bosma and Jonathan Levie, authors of the Global Entrepreneurship Monitor's Executive Report (2009), "A person has a better chance of winning a million dollars or more in a state lottery, than getting venture capital to launch a new business."

In addition to the approximately 28 million businesses in the US today, there are millions more aspiring entrepreneurs. They include students, recent graduates, people working for other companies, those recently laid off, and the recently retired.

People starting and running businesses need all the help they can get. Frankly, it requires knowledge of a wide variety of subjects. Clearly, there is a need for a pragmatic playbook for new and existing entrepreneurs.

Starting from scratch, I cofounded a software company that survived and thrived despite five recessions, four disruptive technology changes, and three huge global competitors. As CEO, I navigated our self-funded company through all seven stages of the business cycle: planning and preparation, start-up, profitability, growth, reinvention, decline, and sale of the company.

I won't say the journey is easy, and I won't say everyone will succeed. In fact, I would say it's extremely challenging. The numbers confirm this: over 50 percent of all new businesses will fail within five years, and 50 percent of the survivors will fail during the following five-year period. The good news is that over time, entrepreneurship provides a level playing field.

As you go out to sell your product or service, no one will ask you if you graduated from Princeton. They will simply ask, "How can you help me?" If you can articulate how you can help and prove it, you can get the order.

There's an entrepreneur inside every one of us. With the right information and knowledge, anyone can start a business and realize his or her dreams. This path to prosperity is available to anyone and everyone who is willing to work hard and work smart.

In the words of Olympic champion Wilma Rudolph, "The potential for greatness lives within each of us."

The goal of *Unlocking Your Entrepreneurial Potential* is to share insights, strategies, and tactics from my thirty-year entrepreneurial career to improve your probability of success, however you may define it. Unlike many books on entrepreneurship that are written by investors, consultants, and academic types, *Unlocking Your Entrepreneurial Potential* is based on practical, real-world experience. I lived it, and I loved it. I hope you will too.

ACKNOWLEDGMENTS

This book would not have been possible without my wife and partner, Laurene. During our twenty-eight-year run at PurchasingNet, Inc., she always had my back. As the company grew, Laurene wore many hats and did many jobs (some very unglamorous, and I thank her for doing them without hesitation), but she never lost her passion for keeping our employees happy and pleasing the customer. Laurene and her team consistently made our customers very happy and reference-able. This allowed me to do my thing. Together we make a great team.

Thanks to our children, Tim Jr. and Erika. You're great kids, and I'm thankful for both of you. You each have a good head on your shoulders, and you made my job as a father easy. This helped me keep my eye on the ball. Erika, we are grateful that you put up with our impromptu nightly meetings at the dinner table. Hopefully you learned something you can put to work someday. Thanks, Tim Jr., for helping us plan for the future and for developing T3 into a great student/athlete.

Thanks to our daughter-in-law, Eileen, who as controller worked hard for many years to help us manage cash flow and keep us honest. You were an absolute whiz at gathering and analyzing data with a moment's notice. You are our unsung hero for all the value you added.

Thanks to our employees, suppliers, and advisors for their hard work and amazing contributions. We are grateful!

Thanks to our accountant and financial advisor, Chuck Woolston, and our attorney, Ira Marcus, for providing great guidance throughout our journey. Also, thanks for your friendship.

Thanks to Anthony Mason of CBS News for taking time out of his insanely busy schedule to write the foreword to *Unlocking Your Entrepreneurial Potential*. Anthony worked with my brother Tom, who died unexpectedly while this book was in the final stages of editing. Tom helped me in so many ways and I miss him every day. May he rest in peace.

And lastly, thanks to the iUniverse team, including Denise, Mara, Terri, Cara, and Kathi, for helping me publish this book. I couldn't have done it without you.

INTRODUCTION

The day I started my first company thirty years ago, I began thinking about writing a book about my entrepreneurial journey. During my twenty-eight years with PurchasingNet, I took notes and saved many of the key documents from each stage of the company's development.

Shortly after selling our company in late 2009, I sorted through more than fifty boxes and filing cabinets in the basement of our house in New Jersey. It was time to retrieve and consolidate my notes and start writing.

As luck would have it, one week later it rained nine inches in two days, the power went out, the sump pumps stopped working, and the basement flooded, destroying the boxes of company records.

Fortunately, I had moved the important notes and documents to the garage the day before the flood! They stayed dry, and I was able to write this book. I'm not a big believer in the saying that "everything happens for a reason," but I believe I was destined to write *Unlocking Your Entrepreneurial Potential.*

This is the book I wish I had during my entrepreneurial journey—part reference guide, part playbook, and part personal memoir. The book describes principles, techniques, strategies, and tactics that I used along the way ... most of them successfully deployed, others not. This book will help entrepreneurs with any type of business avoid the mistakes I made and focus on the strategies and tactics that proved successful.

Some highlights of my entrepreneurial journey:
- Started penniless and ended up with more money than I ever imagined.
- Survived five recessions and four disruptive technology changes over the twenty-eight year history of our software company.
- Developed the first-ever Windows and web-based automated purchasing systems.
- Achieved profitability twenty-two out of twenty-four years after hitting the break-even point.
- As a self-funded, privately owned company, competed successfully with three billion-dollar public companies.

All of this was achieved without third-party funding.

A few statistics: There are approximately 28 million small to medium-sized businesses in the United States, with over 500,000 new businesses being formed every month. More than 99 percent of these businesses will never get third-party funding. Half of all new businesses fail within five years.

This book is intended to help the self-funded entrepreneur unlock his or her entrepreneurial potential. This will improve your probability of success, however you may define it.

Since virtually all new jobs in our economy are created by new small and midsize businesses, this is more than a self-help book. It's a prescription for economic prosperity—for the individual, the United States, and entrepreneurs throughout the world.

Organization of *Unlocking Your Entrepreneurial Potential*

There are seven stages of a successful company's life cycle. They are:

Stage 1.	Preparation and Planning
Stage 2.	Launch through Breakeven
Stage 3.	Achieving and Maintaining Profitability
Stage 4.	Growth
Stage 5.	Reinvention
Stage 6.	Decline (and Cost-Cutting)
Stage 7.	Selling the Company

Almost all entrepreneurial activities can be assigned to one of four categories: Mind-Set, Marketing, Money, and Management. Each of the seven stages of the business life cycle has its own unique strategies and tactics for each of the "Four M's." Each of the stages has a chapter dedicated to Mind-Set, Marketing, Money, and Management.

Dive in anywhere! There's no need to read this book cover to cover. If you are interested only in marketing, read only the marketing chapters in each of the seven stages. Those in the start-up stage might only be interest in chapters pertaining to their situation. Hopefully you will find a few nuggets that will unlock your entrepreneurial potential.

Highlights from *Unlocking Your Entrepreneurial Potential*

The following matrix highlights a critical strategy or tactic for each state of the business cycle. This matrix also describes how *Unlocking Your Entrepreneurial Potential* is organized.

Highlights from Unlocking Your Entrepreneurial Potential: Marketing, Money, and Management Strategies for the Self-Funded Entrepreneur (SFE)

4 M's	Stage 1 Preparation and Planning	Stage 2 Launch through Breakeven	Stage 3 Achieving and Maintaining Profitability	Stage 4 The Growth Stage	Stage 5 The Reinvention Phase	Stage 6 Decline (and Cost-Cutting)	Stage 7 Selling the Company
Mind-Set	• The SFE IQ Test	• The SFE Emotional Roller Coaster	• Lifetime Learning	• Understanding Venture Capitalists	• Understanding Product Life Cycles	• 10 Tips for Dealing with Decline	• Value Drivers
Marketing	• Creating a Product or Service	• Guerilla Marketing	• Sales Methodologies	• Going Global	• 30-Second Elevator Pitch	• Selling More to Existing Customers	• The Language of M&A
Money	• Self-Funding Techniques	• Maximizing Revenues and Minimizing Costs	• Investing 101 for SFEs	• The SFE Reflex Action	• Financial Impact of Reinvention	• Staff Reductions	• Risk vs. Reward Analysis
Management	• Spouses as Partners	• 15 Principles of Hiring Great People	• Building an Organization	• 10 Ways to Deal with SFE Stress	• Board of Advisors	• Forced Ranking	• Closing and Transition

The Fifth M: (Miscellaneous)
- My Top 10 Mulligans
- An Entrepreneur's Prescription for Economic Growth
- Appendix – Sample Letter of Intent and M&A Documents

Now let's begin the journey and unlock your entrepreneurial potential.

STAGE 1:

Preparation and Planning
Mind-Set

| Mind-Set | Marketing | Money | Management |

You gotta make your own kind of music.
Sing your own special song.
Make your own kind of music.
Even if nobody else sings along.

Make Your Own Kind of Music
Written by Barry Mann and Cynthia Weil

There are many reasons for starting a new business. Building wealth, becoming famous, working your own hours, working in your own home, and "changing the world" are all good reasons for starting your own business.

Mine were somewhat different.

I spent eleven years working for large corporations such as IBM, Singer, and Sara Lee. During that time, I learned a lot but felt like I wasn't getting an opportunity to use what I had learned. I wanted to make a difference. Everywhere I turned, I saw too many people doing too little meaningful work.

In my eleven-year corporate career, I held many management positions, including Production and Inventory Control manager and Materials manager. My first job was at IBM as an industrial engineer and later a cost estimator.

1

Anyone who has ever worked for a large organization knows what I'm talking about. There was something about working in this environment that bored and frustrated me.

I don't think I realized it early in my career, but I really needed to do my own thing. I began thinking about starting some kind of a business about five years before I actually made the break.

Don't get me wrong—there were many things I learned along the way that ultimately helped me become a successful entrepreneur. I learned the right way and the wrong way to do things. I certainly received a solid foundation in management, managing both people and money.

For example, at IBM I learned how to treat employees with respect. I also saw a company that had become bloated, a victim of its own success. I used to tell my coworkers and manager that IBM had twice as many employees as it needed. There were 400,000 employees worldwide. Lou Gerstner, IBM's CEO from 1993 to 2002, eventually fixed that problem by cutting the workforce by 40 percent and repositioning the company to sell more services and rely less on hardware revenue.

At Singer, I learned how to introduce and manage change in an old-line organization that was highly resistant to change. I also learned how to manage and motivate people of various backgrounds, points of views, and capabilities. At age twenty-nine, I had 120 people reporting to me. My area of responsibility included both union and nonunion workers. It was a *great* learning experience.

At Sara Lee, I saw how one person could make a difference by taking some risks. This led me to totally automate the manpower-planning process and reduce monthly planning time by 90 percent.

Take-Away #1

Work for one or more companies before starting your own business. You'll learn the right way and the wrong way to do things. These insights will help you build a solid foundation for starting your own business.

Ultimately, my experience in these larger companies inspired me to start my own software company, PurchasingNet, Inc. During my corporate career, I had come to learn firsthand how a purchasing department (sometimes procurement department) functions within a large company. This experience helped me develop personal-computer applications to automate the procurement process in midsized to large companies. (More on this later.)

I acknowledge that when the economy is soft and few jobs are available for recent graduates, there is a temptation to start your own company rather than find a job. Unfortunately, starting a business with no previous business experience is a prescription for disaster for most people. If you do go down this path, make sure you build a business around things you have personally experienced, such as college life, online experiences, or games.

One of the most important things you can do in building your own company is to learn all you can about your potential customers before starting your business. You have to know what makes them tick, what problems they need to solve, and how they go about making decisions.

In our case, I had experienced the challenges of being a procurement manager in a midsized to large company. Procurement managers spent lots of time on routine administrative tasks, lacked timely and accurate information, and were under incredible pressures to get things delivered on time (or early)— all without the lead time or tools to do the job. They were always stressed!

These insights were critical in the formation of our company. After considering a number of other products and services (such as software for hazardous-waste management), we decided to develop a software package we later named P.O. Writer. The original vision was to help purchasing departments automate the preparation of Purchase Orders (POs) and generate meaningful management summary reports.

Our original vision was to replace the typewriters, word processors, filing cabinets, and large mainframe computers used by purchasing departments in the 1980s and '90s.

Reasons for Becoming an Entrepreneur

My original objectives for becoming an entrepreneur were to:

- Create something new, unique, and useful that would improve industrial productivity.
- Stop working in a slow-moving bureaucracy.
- Be independent and control my own destiny.
- Spend less time traveling and commuting. That gets old in a hurry. (At two different times in my career, I commuted five hours a day. I totaled all the time I spent commuting plus working and calculated an hourly rate. At the time, if I could figure out a way to start a business and make ten dollars an hour, I would be way ahead of the game.)
- Apply management skills I had learned working at various companies.
- Do meaningful work.

3

You'll notice that making money was not a motivating force in the beginning. I viewed making money more as a scorekeeping method than a step toward creating great personal wealth.

That changed over time. My secondary objectives became:

- Make a good living and save for retirement.
- Lead a balanced lifestyle.
- Grow the business.
- Eventually sell the business and do something else (like writing this book).

It took twenty-eight years, but we accomplished each of these goals. It was a great ride and rewarding in so many ways. It was by far the greatest experience of my professional life. I hope you get the same opportunity I had. I hope that the things I learned can help you succeed and achieve your goals, whatever they may be.

Dreaming

Don't be afraid to dream about starting different types of businesses. I spent about five years thinking about the kind of business I'd like to own. I ran hundreds of possible scenarios through my mind before starting my initial business: a management consulting company run by myself and a partner.

This thought process will help you get comfortable with the business without starting down the wrong path. By running through all those scenarios in your mind, you will substantially minimize the risk of failure.

> ## Take-Away #2
>
> It's okay to daydream about starting hundreds of businesses before starting your first. In fact, it will help you minimize your risk.

Avoiding Analysis Paralysis

Do you have the courage to make decisions with incomplete data? This is critically important to starting and running a business. An entrepreneur rarely has all the information and data needed to perform a perfect analysis and make the right decision all of the time.

An entrepreneur makes hundreds if not thousands of decisions every day—most with imperfect, incomplete data. In most cases, it is far better to make the best possible decision with 80 percent of the desired data than to wait until all of the data is available to you.

Take-Away #3

You don't need all the facts before starting your business. Sometimes it helps to be a little naïve. If you understood all the risks and how hard it would be, you'd never get started in the first place.

With that said, you will not make the correct decision all the time. One of our mottos at PurchasingNet was, "Progressive improvement beats the hell out of postponed perfection."

After carefully considering the risk of making the wrong decision, plot a course and get started! Naturally, you don't want to get started down a potentially disastrous path, but don't be afraid to start with a small first step that's less than perfect. You can correct or refine your ideas as you move forward. Just think of it as a mid-flight correction.

Many people study things to death. They suffer from "paralysis of analysis" and never get started.

Take-Away #4

Progressive improvement beats the hell out of postponed perfection.

The Four M's

One of the critical activities you'll need to tackle early in the planning process is evaluating your skills, likes, and strengths to see if you have what it takes to launch and build your own enterprise. I like to talk about the Four M's needed by the self-funded entrepreneur. They are Mind-Set, Marketing (including Sales), Money, and Management.

I have found that it is very unusual for a single individual to have adequate knowledge, skills, and experience in each of these areas.

For example, despite my background in two of the Four M's (Management and Money), I had little experience in Marketing, and I wasn't sure if I had the right Mind-Set to succeed.

I teamed up with a colleague at Singer who had a much more outgoing personality and had built good relationships with two well-known MRP consultants. MRP stands for manufacturing resource planning (today known

5

as supply-chain management). These two men, Hal Mather and George Plossl, were internationally known gurus in the industry. I worshipped these guys. Frankly, I'm not sure I could have picked up the phone and talked to either of them without freezing. They were truly icons in the industry, and I was a wannabe.

Hal Mather was originally from the UK. He was a really smart guy and a great speaker. Hal used to speak to large groups around the world on a regular basis. At the time, Hal charged something like $5,000 a day to consult with companies.

Mather and Plossl had just produced a video series that was designed to educate manufacturing people in midsize to large companies. My colleague and I talked Hal Mather into letting us use their video series to conduct training courses at client companies. This provided instant credibility and was a win-win. They would get more exposure for their video series, the client would get hands-on instruction, and we could charge for our services.

So now we were in business. We designed business cards and stationery for our new enterprise. We named it IPM Associates (for inventory production management) and created a crude logo consisting of a triangle with one side each for I, P, and M. Not a thing of beauty, but we were off to the races. It was exhilarating!

But now what?

We decided to mimic the design and format of the newsletter Mather and Plossl published every month. This was a four-page newsletter that was sent out to their mailing list of clients and prospects.

Our newsletter described the education and training services we were providing (or hoped to provide). The Mather and Plossl video series gave us credibility and made us appear bigger and more established than we were. The fact is, we were just starting and had no actual customers.

But we knew we could provide a great service. We had successfully used the video series at multiple companies (as employees) and knew the material inside and out.

We convinced Hal Mather to let us use his mailing list, so we printed a thousand of our newsletters and mailed them out.

A week later, we landed our first customer: a company named Simonds Cutting Tools in Ohio. I began to see how important the sales and marketing process was to starting a new business, and I knew I would need a partner to get this off the ground.

Shortly thereafter, we landed a big deal with National Steel in Houston, Texas. Life was beautiful. We were on top of the world!

As my confidence grew, I started to feel comfortable talking to prospects, and even to George Plossl. George was like a god to me. He started out as partners with the legendary Ollie Wight and helped put MRP (also now known as ERP) on the map. He was known and respected by everyone in the field—and now he would even take my phone calls!

Hal Mather took a liking to me and became a mentor. He showed me the best way to give a presentation to a group ("Never turn out the lights during a presentation, maintain eye contact with several audience members, and above all else … *keep them awake!*").

Hal also encouraged me to write a book to become known in the industry. He agreed to help me edit and publish the book. I ended up writing a takeoff on the popular book of the 1980s called *Up the Organization*, which was authored by Robert Townsend, the CEO of Avis. I loved that book! It was irreverent and humorous, but provided many great insights into big business.

My book was titled, *Up the Manufacturing Organization: The Modern Materials Manager's Guide to Survival.* Hal helped me edit the book. In the process, I learned a lot about writing.

After nine months of writing and editing, Hal decided to go off on his own, so he wouldn't be able to publish the book. This was devastating news for me.

When I asked Hal how I was going to get it published, he looked at me and said, "You can publish it yourself." That led me to form TSM Publishing (my initials) to do just that.

At the time, there weren't any online tools to help people self-publish, so this became a time-consuming task. I found a company that printed books and made a deal with them to print a thousand soft-cover books at a cost of four dollars a book. They agreed to stretch out the payment terms so I could conserve my cash. I hoped that I could sell a few books before I had to make my first payment.

I ended up selling three thousand copies (three printings) and received speaking invitations from sixty different professional organizations throughout the United States. I actually became a mini-celebrity in the industry and formed Tim McEneny, Inc., to provide management-consulting services.

I learned a lot about speaking and became comfortable speaking to groups of five hundred people.

I racked up a ton of air miles and rented Avis cars everywhere I went. (Besides being inspired by their CEO's book, I liked Avis's slogan—"We're number two. We try harder!")

All of this was done while I was still an employee at Singer. Singer had previously announced its intention to shut down the plant in Elizabeth, New Jersey. I worked out a deal with management to take unpaid personal time to start my business while remaining with Singer to help wind down operations at the plant.

> ## Take-Away #5
>
> Start your business while working for someone else. Even if it means working fifteen hours a day, it's the best way to become a self-funded entrepreneur.

I had formed three companies in a space of one year, all while working for another company and still receiving a paycheck. The self-funded entrepreneur was born.

Writing

A skill that is particularly important is the ability to write. If you think about it, the need for good writing touches every part of a business, whether it's writing a brochure, a website, an instruction manual, an e-mail, a proposal, or even a simple business letter. I am constantly amazed at the number of college-educated people who don't have good business-writing skills.

> ## Take-Away #6
>
> Read William Strunk's book *The Elements of Style*. It has been around forever, but it can help you write in a clear, concise manner. This is critical in business.

Flowery, long-winded prose is not appropriate in business writing. Long, rambling paragraphs never get read. At the other end of the spectrum, writing in lowercase, one-syllable words has crept into business-communication styles. This is an unfortunate by-product of texting. It is important to note that writing styles vary depending on the medium—but when in doubt, *keep it short!*

The Self-Funded Entrepreneur's IQ Test

Over 99% of all entrepreneurial ventures never receive third-party funding. This means that the vast majority of entrepreneurs need to self-fund their own companies. To see if you have what it takes to succeed as a self-funded entrepreneur (SFE), take the Self-Funded Entrepreneur's IQ Test.

Objectives of the Self-Funded Entrepreneur's IQ Test:
1. Determine if an individual currently possesses the knowledge, experience, and skills to successfully start and manage his or her own business.
2. Identify areas needing improvement before starting a business.
3. Assess if an individual should have partners or outside expertise in the new venture—and if so, what those partners' strengths should be.
4. Determine the type of business at which an individual can excel.
5. Determine how an entrepreneur currently running a business can improve the performance of the business.

Instructions:
- Answer all questions (if you don't have the patience, you probably won't be a successful self-funded entrepreneur).
- Don't be afraid to admit you don't know something (be honest).
- If you find you're very weak in one area, don't stop taking the test (everyone has weaknesses).
- Each question should be answered with a score of 0 (least) to 10 (most). Average would be in the range of 4–6, good 7–8, and excellent 9–10. Poor would be 0–3. If you're not sure, guess! It's not critical to be precise with each answer.
- No questions are "make it or break it" questions.
- The sum of the fifty questions represents your total SFE IQ Score.

The SFE IQ Test covers the Four M's of entrepreneurship:
- Mind-Set
- Marketing
- Money
- Management

… plus ten Miscellaneous intangibles.

No.	SFE's IQ Test—MIND-SET Rate 0 (Least) to 10 (Most)	Score
1	Quality and quantity of formal education (regardless of area of concentration)	
2	Quality of work experience (regardless of amount and area of expertise)	
3	Relevance of work experience (relevant to your new business)	
4	Time spent reading and learning outside of work/school in a typical week (a score of 10 would be 10 or more hours a week)	
5	Number of months you could go without a paycheck and still pay your bills (10 is the highest possible score)	
6	Clear vision of the future (of your business)	
7	Analytical skills (can identify problems and lay out a course of corrective action)	
8	Resourcefulness (creative problem-solving skills)	
9	Ability to go without immediate feedback from other people (long-term orientation)	
10	Ability to work without well-defined policies and procedures (can "make it up" as you go)	
	Overall Score:	

No.	SFE's IQ Test—MARKETING Rate 0 (Least) to 10 (Most)	Score
1	Knowledge of direct-mail and e-mail marketing techniques	
2	Firsthand knowledge of your chosen marketplace	
3	Experience with online and print advertising (creation and placement)	
4	Business writing skills	
5	Effectiveness making oral presentations	
6	Knowledge of the Four Ps of marketing	
7	Can define your "unique selling proposition"	
8	Can explain the difference between marketing and sales	
9	Knowledge of technology (including search-engine optimization and use of social networks) and how it can be used to improve marketing/sales activities	
10	Can define your sales methodology	
	Overall Score:	

No.	SFE's IQ Test—MONEY Rate 0 (Least) to 10 (Most)	Score
1	If a saver is a 10 and a spender is a 0, I am a …	
2	Can define P&L	
3	Can calculate a break-even point	
4	Know the difference between cash basis of accounting and accrual method, and when each is appropriate	
5	Know the fundamental equation of a balance sheet	
6	Can explain the difference between equity and debt financing	
7	Can explain the time value of money	
8	Can define "gross margin"	
9	Know what a "chart of accounts" is	
10	Know the theory of sunk costs	
	Overall Score:	

No.	SFE's IQ Test —MANAGEMENT Rate 0 (Least) to 10 (Most)	Score
1	Know how to hire the right people	
2	Know how to plan and execute a layoff	
3	Have good time-management skills	
4	Know what KPI stands for	
5	Have a good "feel" for numbers	
6	Have good negotiating skills	
7	Management experience—number of years with people reporting to you (maximum score of 10)	
8	Can speak extemporaneously in front of people	
9	Know how to implement and use technology to manage a business	
10	Use risk-reward analysis for making decisions	
	Overall Score:	

No.	SFE's IQ Test—Miscellaneous Intangibles Rate 0 (Least) to 10 (Most)	Score
1	Self-confidence in a business environment	
2	Planning skills	
3	Multitasking abilities	
4	Competitiveness and persistence	
5	Willingness/ability to devote three years of your life to starting a business (everything else becomes secondary)	
6	Willingness do whatever it takes to succeed (can overcome adversity)	
7	Ability to ignore what others think	
8	Ability to overcome fear of failure	
9	Enjoys taking risks and can afford to	
10	Entrepreneurial family	
	Overall Score: **NOTE**: For an unbiased rating, try having a business associate answer 1–7.	

	SFE's IQ TEST SUMMARY
	Score
Mind-Set	
Marketing	
Money	
Management	
Miscellaneous	
TOTAL SCORE	

How to Interpret the SFE's IQ Test Results

• 90 or over in a single category	Excellent probability of success in this area.
• 80–90 in a single category	Acceptable, but needs improvement.
• Under 80	Need a partner with strengths in this area or a close relationship with someone outside the company who can help you.

Age Thirty-Two—The Perfect Age to Start a Business

Let's face it: you're still growing up when you're in your twenties. You're maturing mentally and emotionally during this time and aren't ready to start a business unless you are truly gifted, have lots of connections, and can get your hands on lots of money. Stories about Bill Gates, Michael Dell, and Mark Zuckerberg are legendary ... and mostly true. But the probability of the typical entrepreneur having these attributes (as well as the great sense of timing) is practically zero.

I became a self-funded entrepreneur when I was thirty-two. For me, that was the right time. I had received all of the formal education I could stand (and afford), and I had learned firsthand how the business world really worked.

Regarding formal education, I always recommend people get as much as they can stand and as much as they can afford. I was lucky enough to attend Lehigh University in Bethlehem, Pennsylvania, where I received a bachelor of science degree in industrial engineering. I remember having a professor who said, "Half of what we're teaching will be obsolete in ten years. The problem is that we don't know which half!" In reality, I think it turned out to be more like 80 percent of what they taught was already obsolete or irrelevant to me at the time.

Academic institutions always lag behind the true needs of the business world, and Lehigh was no exception. What I did learn (and use every day of my life) is how to analyze and solve problems. This skill is essential for would-be entrepreneurs. You will be faced with hundreds of problems every day that will need solving. To me, this is the real value of a formal education.

Harvard, Penn, and Stanford are the cream of the crop when it comes to business. There are many fine colleges and universities, but none quite like these three when it comes to networking in the business world. Graduates from these institutions have a truly special bond. Investment banking, venture capital, private equity, technology, consulting, and a number of other industries are dominated by graduates from these three universities. I always have believed that the only real value of an MBA was getting your next job—unless you go to Harvard, Penn, or Stanford. These three will help open doors for the rest of your life.

Take-Away #7

Get as much formal education as you can stand and can afford.

The other reason to wait to start your own business is that this time can be used to save as much money as possible before starting up. PurchasingNet was started with a small investment savings accumulated from the age of twenty-one to thirty-two.

Fortunately, in today's world, many businesses can be started for very little money. At a minimum, however, you will still need money for a website, phones, and building an organization. It is also advisable to have at least a six-month emergency fund built up before starting.

More importantly, this time will help you learn about your potential customers and what their needs are. This is extremely important for any self-funded entrepreneur. *Know your market cold!* I am not a big fan of focus groups; they tend to reveal customer wants and needs, but not necessarily ideas for products and services that people are willing to pay for. These are best discovered by working in and around potential customers and decision makers. So if you want to start a landscaping business, work for an established landscaping company (or two) to learn about customer expectations.

> ## Take-Away #8
>
> The perfect age to start a business is thirty-two. You're old enough to know what you don't know but still young enough to think you can do anything.

Investing time to learn as much as you can about your marketplace is critical to a successful launch. Think about the marketplace first and *then* consider the type of product or service you would like to offer. It's all about meeting customer needs, not just picking a product or service *you* think is cool.

Some people make the mistake of trying to pick a product or service they think is cool or important, and then they try to figure out how they can sell it. This is exactly the wrong approach.

Here are ten questions you should be able to answer before picking a product or service to sell.

1. Who is my potential marketplace?

2. Do I have a firsthand understanding of the marketplace?

3. What are my potential customers' problems and needs?

4. What are their areas of pain?

5. Would they be willing to pay to have these problems solved and their pain relieved, and who would make the decision to spend the money?

6. What alternatives exist today to meet these needs?

7. Who are the potential competitors in the space today?

8. What are their strengths and weaknesses?

9. What are the opportunities to better meet the needs of the marketplace?

10. Can you provide a better product or service at a reasonable price (your unique selling proposition)?

Only after these questions have been answered can you begin thinking about a specific product or service to sell.

In our case, we answered these questions this way:

Q1.   Who is my potential marketplace?
   A.   Purchasing departments of midsize to large companies.

Q2.   Do I have a firsthand understanding of the marketplace?
   A.   I had worked in and around purchasing departments for eleven years.

Q3.   What are my potential customers' problems and needs?
   A.   A lack of tools to automate purchasing transactions (POs) and a lack of timely, accurate information to negotiate lower prices.

Q4.   What are their areas of pain?
   A.   Purchasing departments are under the gun to ensure on-time delivery of goods and services. Everyone from the maintenance guy to the CEO is constantly pressuring buyers to expedite orders.

Q5.   Would they be willing to pay to have these problems solved and their pain relieved, and who would make the decision to spend the money?
   A.   We believed they would pay for a solution and that the director of purchasing alone could approve the purchase of a solution if it was within his or her signing authority. (Later we learned that IT and finance executives also had to buy in.)

Q6.   What alternatives exist today to meet these needs?
   A.   There were word-processing solutions, spreadsheet solutions, and mainframe software solutions available that addressed a small fraction of the pain. Purchasing executives had to beg and cajole IT management to deliver one of these solutions. It usually involved some degree of custom programming, and the purchasing department was very low on the priority list. (We actually built an entire marketing campaign around the purchasing department being thirteenth on IT's priority list.)

Q7.	Who are the potential competitors in the space today?
　　　A.	At the time, there was only one other PC-based purchasing software package available. Most of the purchasing systems were "homegrown" mainframe systems.

Q8.	What are their strengths and weaknesses?
　　　A.	Our competitor had completed their IPO (initial public offering), was well-financed (raised about $5 million), and had the backing of the ISM (then NAPM), the professional society for purchasing executives. Their weakness was that their product offering wasn't very good. It was very simplistic and had limited use in the real world.

Q9.	What are the opportunities to better meet the needs of the marketplace?
　　　A.	We had the real-world knowledge to "build a better mousetrap" that addressed more of the needs and pains of the typical purchasing department.

Q10.	Can you provide a better product or service at a reasonable price?
　　　A.	Initially we believed we could sell a comprehensive, PC-based purchasing software package for under $2,000. Our unique selling proposition was a system developed "For Purchasing People, by Purchasing People."

And so we began to formulate plans for designing and building a PC-based purchasing system.

Take-Away #9

The best way for the average person to build wealth and gain independence is to start a business. You'll never get rich working for someone else.

Buying a Franchise versus Creating a Unique Product or Service

Make an honest self-assessment to determine the right type of business for you. Are you a creative person? Are you a leader or follower? Can you start with a blank piece of paper and write something meaningful and effective? Are you versatile (think of the Four M's)? How did you fare on the Self-Funded Entrepreneur's IQ Test?

The answers to these questions will help you decide whether to buy a franchise or create your own business from scratch. Here is the spectrum of entrepreneurial choices:

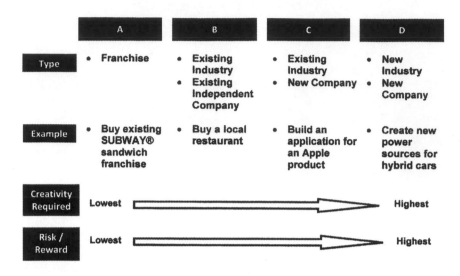

At the lowest end of the graphic, buying an existing franchise minimizes risk. There's an established company with established products/services and established marketing programs. Tactical skills are required to be successful (such as sales, customer service, and maintenance). However, proven processes and products limit the creativity required.

On the highest end of the graphic, creating a new business in a new industry represents more risk but with a higher possible reward.

Starting or buying an independent company in an established industry falls somewhere in the middle.

In addition to the factors mentioned, the amount of capital available is always a significant factor for the self-funded entrepreneur. There is not necessarily a correlation between the type of business and the capital required. A Burger King franchise might cost a million dollars but have very predictable profitability. Developing an app for Apple's iPad might require $10,000 or less, but it may generate very little revenue and ultimately fail.

The "Two out of Three" Rule

To play the game in any competitive market, you've got to beat the existing competition in at least two out of three categories:

- Service
- Quality
- Price

It doesn't matter if you're a Chinese restaurant, a software company, or a home builder, if you can't be very competitive in at least two out of three categories, you won't make it. If you are better than your competitors in all three categories, you have a great chance of being very successful. The determining factors will then become the Four M's—but if you don't pass the "two out of three" test, you won't have a chance.

Service is determined by the overall customer experience and the level of customer satisfaction, including timely delivery of the product or service.

Quality is determined by the reliability, consistency, and durability of your product or service.

Price is the total net price of your product or service. Value received by the customer is critical.

It should be noted that you don't need to be the best in all three areas to succeed. In fact, many successful small businesses sell based on superior quality and service but have slightly higher prices than their competition. Many customers are willing to pay more for great service and quality.

For example, our annual software support and maintenance fees were 25 to 33 percent of the original license fee, versus the competition's 15 to 20 percent. This helped expand our margins and make us a more profitable company. Of course, we needed to provide excellent service and consistently offer quality upgrades to justify our higher prices.

Where Does Capital Come From?

Some people are of the opinion that they can take their idea for a new business to a bank and get a loan to finance their start-up.

This is an unlikely scenario.

A banker needs more than a passionate entrepreneur-to-be to make a loan, even with an SBA (Small Business Administration) guarantee. "Free" government grants are also unlikely.

It is far more productive to start your business and generate some revenue (or at least firm orders) from real customers before seeking a loan or third-party funding of any type. This adds credibility and minimizes risk for both you and the banker.

Even if you start with a small subset of products or services selling to a small subset of your eventual marketplace, gaining some actual experience with your idea will give a prospective lender some comfort. This is referred to as a lean start-up, pilot project, proof of concept, or controlled rollout.

Take-Away #10

Orders first. Loans second.

Over 500,000 businesses are started every month in the United States. Less than 1 percent of these receive funding from third-party sources. The other 99 percent are led by self-funded entrepreneurs. Let's review the potential sources of capital for the self-funded entrepreneur (SFE):

1. Savings generated while working for other companies. If you're just out of school and starting to work, keep this in mind: the primary source of start-up capital will be your savings. Try not to withdraw retirement or 401(k) savings, especially if you're over fifty. If you are unemployed and feel you won't be able to get a new job but still need income, look at using a small portion of your 401(k) to fund your new venture. If you do decide to withdraw money from your 401(k), make sure you comply with all IRS requirements.

2. Money made during the start-up phase while working for your current employers. Never quit your current job while starting up a new company! Line up at least one or two paying customers before you make the break.

3. Money made by your spouse or partner while you are starting the new business.

4. Personal overhead and expense reduction. This is no time to buy a fancy new car or take an exotic vacation! Personal sacrifices may be required to fund your new business. Laurene and I even returned many of our wedding gifts to stay afloat.

5. Money loaned or gifted by relatives. This is a very tricky area and should not be pursued if it could cause conflict within the family. Better to stay away from this option.

6. Home-equity loans on your residence. Be careful! If you feel comfortable with this option, it can provide capital or a safety net, but it adds to your debt load and risk because it is secured by your home.

7. Managing cash flow. (More on this later.)

There are stories about entrepreneurs who started their companies with credit cards. In this day and age, this is not advisable because the costs are too high (20 percent interest or higher) and the risks are too high.

Creative Problem-Solving

Entrepreneurs are very creative problem-solvers. If you're not, you'll need a partner who is.

Some of the principles of entrepreneurial problem-solving are:

1. Your proposed solution doesn't have to be perfect! It should move you in the right direction quickly, however.

It is more important to address the problem in a timely fashion, before it becomes a bigger problem. Speed is more important than the elegance of your solution.

As it relates to product development, we used the philosophy of "Go ugly, early." This enabled us to get a software product out into the real world quickly and receive actual feedback from real paying customers. We would then incorporate these changes as quickly as possible to improve our products.

I always say that if you can address and solve 80 percent of the problem proactively, it's far better than waiting until you've pondered the solution for days, weeks, or months in hopes of finding the perfect answer.

Problems will be coming at you so fast once you start your business that if you insist on a 100 percent solution, you'll become the "deer in the headlights" and never accomplish anything. Remember this motto: "Progressive improvement beats the hell out of postponed perfection."

Take-Away #11

Go ugly, early. Speed is more important than the elegance of your solution.

---

2. Think of a pyramid when problem solving:

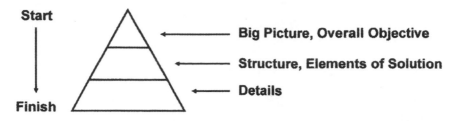

It is important to start at the top of the pyramid with the big picture and overall objective. What are you trying to achieve? Moving down the pyramid, you can then address the "how to" and finally figure out the supporting details.

Don't fall into the trap of starting with the details without first knowing where you want to end up. You should know how the customer will benefit by your solution before moving down the pyramid.

3. Break down problems before trying to solve them.

Many times a big problem is comprised of multiple smaller problems that can and should be solved separately.

An example might be a product or service that isn't selling as much as expected. In order to determine why the product isn't selling, you need to examine the contributing factors to figure out how each can be improved.

Perhaps the product itself can be improved, the position of the product can be modified, or the price can be adjusted (up or down). Perhaps the sales script needs to be improved or more education and training may be required for the sales force. It is possible that only one of these four factors needs to be addressed. Perhaps multiple factors need to be addressed.

You must complete this analysis before plotting a course of action. Just trying harder to sell the product is not going to help you achieve your objective.

Business Plans

The business plan is one of the most overrated documents I know. Countless books have been written about how to create the perfect business plan. Software is available to help entrepreneurs create an elaborate business plan.

Don't waste your time or money trying to create a fancy business plan. Why?

First, business plans and the assumptions that go into them will change the day after the plan is published. It is far more important to have a Plan B in mind when conditions change. What will you do when one of your assumptions or forecasts proves to be inaccurate?

Second, the only reason to create an elaborate business plan is to attract outside investors. It's too early for the self-funded entrepreneur to look for outside funding. Use your time and effort to get the business off the ground.

Third, you should already have a plan for your business in your head, one that goes out one or two years. This should include your projection of cash flow, product plans, partnerships, marketing plans, hiring plans, and resource requirements. These factors will always be changing, and customer feedback will create a dynamic environment. Despite my disdain for the business plan as a formal *document*, the business-planning *process* can be quite valuable if it becomes a business replanning process and keeps up with the velocity of the business.

Fourth, people don't have time to read long, elaborate business plans. You can develop ten PowerPoint slides to convey the important points, objectives, and milestones. This format is far more likely to get read than a thirty-page business plan or offering memorandum.

Take-Away #12

Always have a Plan B in your hip pocket. The assumptions in a business plan will prove to be wrong.

Fifth, the important part of business planning is not the elaborate five-year plan with a "hockey stick" forecast; it's the thought process that has gotten you to this point. Some of the great business plans of all time were written on cocktail napkins or paper placemats—Dell Computer and PurchasingNet, Inc., to name two.

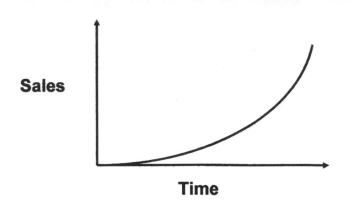

"Hockey Stick" Forecast

We found that it usually takes three times as much money (and time) to reach the break-even point than anticipated. Business plans tend to be overly optimistic, and any potential investor or acquirer knows it.

Take-Away #13

You can count on spending three times more money than you originally planned to reach the break-even point and become profitable.

Will It to Happen

Sometimes when starting a business, it is actually helpful *not* to have all the answers. Being a little naïve can be a positive. We often said that if we knew everything involved in starting and running a business, we never would have started it in the first place.

You can overcome a lack of information by working passionately every day. When I say every day, I mean *every day*. This requires a 365-days-a-year commitment, at least until you pass the break-even point.

At the end of each day, you should ask yourself, "How did I move the company forward today?" Even if you could only put in three or four hours on a Sunday because of family obligations, your goal should be to get enough done to move the company closer to launch or whatever the next milestone may be.

I don't mean to imply that you need to work fifteen hours each day, but each day that passes without accomplishing anything is a day you can't get back. Time is the only thing you can't replenish.

Starting a new business is, in fact, a hell of a lot of work. Fortunately, most of the time, you're really excited and running on adrenaline. In the end, it is worth every minute of effort expended.

What Do You Want to Accomplish?

Some people start and build a company with an IPO as the desired endgame. They build their companies to grow quickly, hoping to cash out once the company completes its IPO. During the 1980s, '90s, and a few years after that, this was an achievable scenario, and many company founders accomplished their dreams.

One of PurchasingNet's biggest competitors during the start-up, breakeven, and growth phases was a company called Greentree Software. Greentree went public early on, had about a fifteen-year lifespan, and raised a total of $25 million during its life cycle.

I ran into Greentree's CEO at a trade show where our companies were both exhibiting. He was very good at getting outside funding but not too strong on managing the business. He said to me, "Hey Tim, you ought to take your company public so you can deposit some money in the 'hip national bank,'" as he slapped his wallet.

He was obviously very pleased that he had pocketed part of the proceeds from their IPO, all legal and aboveboard.

Our objectives and goals were different. At PurchasingNet, we wanted to build a high-quality, customer-focused, profitable company that would last. We wanted to make a decent living but weren't thinking in terms of a one-time windfall.

Take-Away #14

There's got to be a *mentality* before there's a *reality*.
　　　　　　　　—Raheem Morris, Tampa Bay Buccaneers Head Coach

Some people referred to us as a "lifestyle company." This always ruffled my feathers. We ran PurchasingNet like a business and achieved 21 percent compound growth over the twenty-eight-year life-cycle of the company. The term "lifestyle company" implies that the owners want to make just enough to live (and support their lifestyle) and reinvest very little in the business. Some people refer to this as "buying yourself a job."

Greentree Software, the company that had raised $25 million, had just two profitable years in its history. PurchasingNet, on the other hand, was profitable twenty-two of the next twenty-four years after breaking even.

The self-funded entrepreneur, although an underdog, can compete with public companies.

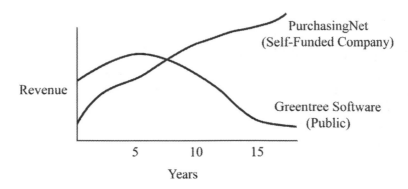

We competed successfully by developing a better product and providing exceptional customer service … and we started with a low, five-figure investment using our own money. Capital isn't everything; it's only one piece of the puzzle.

In today's world (2011 and beyond), the rules of the game are quite a bit different. Institutional investors won't take a chance on a small company with a story, a "hockey stick" forecast, no profits, and no revenues. (In the 1990s, more than a few "pre-revenue" companies IPOed! A book written by Philip J. Kaplan in the early 2000s called *F'd Companies: Spectacular Dot-Com Flameouts* provides an entertaining overview of this period in our history.)

Institutional investors (such as venture capitalists and private-equity investors) want to make sure they minimize their own risks. As a result, they are looking for companies with real products, real customers, revenue growth, and profitability before investing a penny in a new venture.

That doesn't mean you can't start out as a self-funded entrepreneur and seek outside funding down the line to fuel growth and company expansion. The point is, you need to remove as much risk as possible to attract an investor.

Some have called this a "lean start-up," where you develop a subset of your product or service and generate real revenues and positive cash flow before seeking outside investment. This acts as a "proof of concept" for the potential investor and minimizes the risk.

Networking—A Weak Link for Us

Part of being a successful entrepreneur is learning from your mistakes. We could have, and should have, done a much better job of networking. I'm not just talking about online networking; I'm talking about getting to know people who could have helped us increase the value of our company. The people we needed to network with included:

- Bankers
- Publishers, editors, and writers of relevant magazines and newspapers
- Business partners (who could recommend or resell our products)
- Potential investors
- Potential acquirers (including the competition)
- Industry analysts
- Others (such as local organizations)

We tended to be internally focused and customer-focused and only started looking for these folks when we thought we needed them. At the time, we didn't see the value of investing the time in networking. We were too busy doing other things (like running the company and raising a family).

Start Small

One of the criticisms of self-funded entrepreneurs is that we don't think big enough. It's not that we don't think big, it's just that we start small and build on our success.

Part of the self-funded entrepreneur's philosophy is that it's good to take a long-term view of business. There's no need to hit monthly or quarterly forecasts. This is certainly not true of a public company.

The SFE attitude is that it's better to own 100 percent of something small than 1 percent of something big. Control and independence are so important!

So don't be afraid to start small and build on your success. It will help build the foundation of a strong, sustainable company.

Take-Away #15

Start small. Even a small failure can lead to a huge success sometime in the future.

Getting Started

At a minimum, you'll want to file a DBA (doing business as), open a bank account, and get a company phone number. All of this can be done for less than $100.

For more legal protection, you'll want to consider forming an LLC (limited liability corporation) or a corporation. This is handled differently by each state. You must have a unique name for your company (within your state). This can be checked online or through an attorney.

STAGE 1:

Preparation and Planning

Marketing

| Mind-Set | Marketing | Money | Management |

The second of the Four M's is Marketing. Without Marketing, survival is difficult.

Marketing is more than just designing brochures and websites. In fact, Marketing (with a capital M) is the driver for the Four Ps. They are:

- Product (or Service)—What features and functions does the buyer need?
- Pricing—How should we charge our customers?
- Positioning—How does the product or service compare to others?
- Promotion—How can we tell the marketplace about our product?

If you have selected the franchise option, most of these will already be thought out, and you will be given access to the available products and their pricing policies.

For those creating your own products, after you've evaluated the needs of the marketplace, the question is what unique products and services are needed to meet these needs.

Market-driven companies focus their energies on problems that buyers are willing to spend money to solve. First, understand market problems; next, build the products people want to buy; finally, communicate to buyers an understanding of their problems. After that, everything else falls into place.

The best self-funded entrepreneurs create solutions that are narrow and deep. They organize around a single market problem and solve it completely with a solution that handles all related tasks in one easy step. A very small specialized market can yield big profits. Thinking small can yield big rewards.

Selecting a Product or Service

If you have decided to sell products created by someone else, you'll want to identify various sources for these products and analyze their prices, delivery times, quality, supplier stability, and customer service policies. Make sure to check references before making any final decisions.

Creating a Product or Service

When I started my first business, a management consulting firm, I did a lot of traveling. Because of my loyalty to Avis Car Rental, I went through the same process every time I rented a car. I would simply go to the counter and hand over my license and credit card, and within seconds I would be handed a multipage contract with all the data that pertained to me and my car rental.

One night, as I stood watching the impact printer print my rental contract, it suddenly occurred to me: why couldn't this same concept (and technology) be utilized to print a multipart purchase-order form? Most of the data on a Purchase Order could be retrieved from a database storing recent purchases of the same or similar items. Management summary reports could also be run on a regular basis. P.O. Writer (the software product) was born that very night.

The emerging technology of the day was the personal computer. We were convinced it was more than a toy and would eventually be used in corporations of all sizes to solve serious business problems. Today's parallel might be smartphones and tablets replacing personal computers in major corporations. It's not a certainty, but it is a possibility.

We decided to create a software package that could be used by purchasing departments and run on these new personal computers. We had identified a proven solution (used by Avis to print rental contracts) and adapted it to run on a new platform to solve an entirely different problem.

Another example of this approach was used by a man named Forrest Bird of Stoughton, Massachusetts. He invented the modern medical respirator. His invention has given the breath of life to countless people around the world. Bird got his idea through his knowledge of aviation. "In the human lung, there are millions of air foils just like airplane wings. They facilitate normal breathing. I just applied my knowledge of how air goes over the wings of my airplane to solve this problem."

These are examples of how you can create a new product or service. You can adapt an existing solution for use in a different area. This approach has been used by many inventors and businessmen to launch new companies.

Take-Away #16

A great way to start a new business is to apply a proven technology or solution to *your* area of expertise.

We were at a very early phase of a significant *megatrend* (a term popularized by author John Naisbitt in his 1988 book) that lasted many years: the PC. By making this part of our solution, we positioned ourselves for future growth.

Pricing

There's a tendency for all entrepreneurs to price their products too low. In particular, don't undervalue your services—people will pay for great service.

Probably the single most important factor in pricing your product or service is what the market will bear. Customer expectations are all-important when developing a pricing scheme. Your out-of-pocket costs are a factor, but only a secondary concern when establishing pricing. The marketplace will dictate your maximum pricing. Hopefully you have selected a product or service with enough margin to make a profit. If not, it's time to move in a different direction.

Positioning

As a small company, you must have a unique selling proposition. How do you differentiate yourself from the big guys? Why is your product or service unique?

Perhaps you will differentiate yourself on price, quality, service, or markets served.

Markets served can be based on geographic areas or vertical markets. A vertical market is a group of similar companies and customers with specialized needs. These are sometimes referred to as *niche markets*.

Competitors can match your price, quality, or customer service rather easily. With a few organizational changes and a little PR, competitors can close the gap in these areas. That's why it is important to offer a truly unique product or service that can't be duplicated easily.

Your geographic markets (city, county, state, region, country) can be more difficult to penetrate and may require a larger investment on the part of your competitors.

But the best positioning is to serve a specific vertical market or industry category. If you can tailor your product or service to meet the specific needs of a vertical market and dominate that market, you will have built a position that is very difficult to penetrate.

In our case, we targeted purchasing departments in legal and financial-service vertical markets. We ended up virtually owning the legal market (we licensed our software to sixteen of the top twenty-five law firms in the United States). We became known as the procurement experts for law firms. Word of mouth took over, and we found new sales were easier to make as a result of our perceived expertise in this market.

We actually didn't have to change our standard product to serve this vertical market, we just had to demonstrate how the product would meet needs unique to law firms. Our sales people learned the lingo used by law firms. They learned how to use the software to solve firms' unique problems such as billing back as much cost as possible to a particular Client Matter Number, which increased the client's PPP (profit per partner, a key metric in that market).

This type of positioning will create a product offering that is least susceptible to competitive threats. You may think that you will be limiting your overall sales potential by positioning your company with a vertical orientation, but in the long run, it creates a very strong, sustainable company. It also helps minimize sales and marketing costs if you focus your resources on one or two vertical markets. You can still make sales to customers not in your vertical markets. You just aren't spending much money to promote the company or product to serve other markets. You've got to pick your fights in order to succeed in the long term.

Take-Away #17

If you can dominate a vertical market, it will be very difficult for competitors to beat you in that market.

Promotion

Promotional planning at this stage should be limited to designing a plan to test your ideas in the real world before committing your money to the new venture. How do you know if your ideas are good ones? Will customers actually pay money to buy your products and services?

Testing Your Ideas

We had decided to develop a PC-based purchasing software package. Before committing significant resources to build out the product, we wanted to test our idea. At this point, we had just started to develop the product.

We tested our idea by writing a one-page letter describing our software and the benefits it could bring to the typical purchasing department. We included a postage-paid business-response card so recipients could indicate if they were interested and would like to receive more information.

We managed to get our hands on a mailing list of purchasing managers at companies located within a 200-mile radius. We sent a mailing to about 250 people. We rented a post-office box at nearby Troy, Michigan. We mailed all 250 pieces and anxiously waited to see the results.

One of my partners and I drove to the Troy Post Office a week later. I was driving and dropped him off to go check the PO box.

My heart was pounding as I anxiously awaited the results. Did anyone care about our idea? Would anyone be willing to spend money to solve this problem?

Don returned to the car with a very sad look. He glumly reported that he didn't see one response card in the PO box.

I was very disappointed.

He sat in the passenger seat and stared straight ahead in a bit of a trance. We both sighed and prepared to drive off when Don reached into his suit jacket and began to mumble something.

"I didn't see one response card, I saw twelve response cards!" He grabbed them from inside his sport-coat pocket and tossed them in the air as if they were confetti on New Year's Eve.

This translated to almost a 5 percent positive response rate. Of course we were ecstatic.

The normal success rate for direct response marketing is less than 1 percent. The 5 percent response rate greatly exceeded our expectations and provided the validation we needed to take the next step.

The total cost of the testing phase was less than $250 (today it could be done for even less using e-mail). This process showed us that the risks of proceeding were acceptable, and the potential rewards were great.

This technique should be used by every self-funded entrepreneur before moving to the start-up phase. Using online tools, this process can be conducted quickly for very little money. Don't skip this step.

We were now moving forward with great confidence and enthusiasm. Full speed ahead!

Take-Away #18

Evaluate risk versus potential reward before making a decision. Entrepreneurs only take risks if potential rewards outweigh the risks.

The Name Game

Naturally, we had to pick a company name and a product name.

We took about fifteen minutes sitting at the kitchen table one night to pick our initial names: American Tech, Inc., and P.O. Writer. The names lasted about fifteen years. Our next iteration was PurchasingNet, Inc., and PNet. (More on the second iteration later.)

Descriptive versus Nonspecific Names

There are two schools of thought on company and product naming.

The first is to select a name that doesn't tell people anything about the company or product, something like Acropolis LLC. You can't tell anything about the company from the name, but it is distinctive and gives a positive impression. LLC stands for limited liability company, a very popular company structure for SFE's.

The second school of thought is to name the company or product that in some way describes what you do—Pete's Limo LLC, for example.

Perhaps a hybrid naming strategy, such as Acropolis Limo LLC, might incorporate the best of both worlds.

I believe small start-up companies should favor the descriptive name strategy. The reason? You want customers and prospects to instantly know what you do. Larger companies can afford to pick an abstract name and spend large sums of money to build brand awareness (like Accenture, Apple, Avis). The real key, regardless of your naming strategy, is to make sure people can remember your name! You can pick the coolest-sounding name in the world, but it won't work if no one can remember it.

Another consideration is how you will appear in directories. One good thing about the name American Tech was that we usually appeared at the top of the alphabetical listing of procurement software in places like trade magazines and listings.

Search-Engine-Friendly Names

Google has a free tool that can help you learn about the most frequently searched phrases that relate specifically to your product, service, or industry.

By having a company name that aligns with a popular search word or phrase, you will be more likely to appear toward the top of the natural or free listings generated by the search engines. Of course, there are many other factors that search engines take into account to determine their ultimate ranking, but "SEO friendly" (SEO stands for search-engine optimization) company and product names can get you moving in the right direction—toward the top of the list.

Take-Away #19

Read the book *SEO Made Simple* by Michael Fleischner. It is a fast read and can help you think about good names for your product or business.

One Name Fits All

For the small start-up company, a single name for a website domain name (URL), company name, and product name is ideal.

You'll need to check on domain-name availability (I use *www.GoDaddy.com*). For company-name availability, check with the appropriate state government agency (typically the secretary of state). There are Internet sites available to assist with company-name search too (including *www.DirectIncorporation.com* and *www.sbresources.com*).

Product names can be trademarked (™) or slogan marked (℠), so you'll have to perform an online trademark search to check for possible conflicts before determining a product name.

Ideally, you will be able to use the same name for each purpose (company, product, and domain). This allows you to promote one name, not two or three, saving money and eliminating possible confusion in the marketplace.

Sales Channels

In most cases, the self-funded entrepreneur is going to sell his or her own product.

Looking into the future, you may decide to continue selling your product directly to the customer. Another possible strategy would be to use agents, representatives, and franchisees to sell your product.

Generally speaking, the more complex the product or service, the higher the likelihood you'll want (need) to continue to sell directly.

If, however, the product or service is easily understood and explained, there is a higher probability that you can leverage other sales channels. The more commodity-like your product is, the more it lends itself to third-party sales.

The only reason to think about this topic at this stage is so you can develop a product-development strategy consistent with longer term goals. If you're only going to sell through third parties, the product should be simple and easy to understand.

STAGE 1:

Preparation and Planning

Money

The legendary Jack Welch, former CEO of GE, has said that there are three things you need to focus on to build a successful business. They are:

1. Cash Flow
2. Happy Customers
3. Engaged Employees

There are many different ways to measure the financial performance of a company. Public companies report net income (or profit and loss) and balance-sheet data (assets and liabilities) on a quarterly basis.

By far, the most important measurement for the self-funded entrepreneur is cash flow. Simply stated, this measures the actual cash flowing into the company from real customers and compares it to the cash being paid out to employees, suppliers, etc.

Cash Is King

Cash is the lifeblood of any company, big or small. Never forget that!

Larry Garlick, former CEO of a large public software company, once told me, "The only money that really counts is the money paid to you by your customers when they buy your products. Don't confuse that with the money given to you by investors when trying to gauge the health of your company."

The name of the game is generating positive cash flow every year. As long

37

as your enterprise can consistently generate positive cash flow, you will stay out of trouble.

For the first couple of years, most self-funded service-industry start-ups can run their businesses out of their checkbooks. A notable exception would be a construction or manufacturing company where you need to track costs by project or job.

Don't concern yourself with fancy accounting methods like GAAP (generally accepted accounting principles), revenue recognition, and mark-to-market. These will come later as you prepare to sell your company (or if you decide to make the move from being a self-funded entrepreneur to a third-party-funded entrepreneur).

Concentrate on cash flow. You can run your business and pay your taxes just fine using the cash basis of accounting.

Selecting an Accountant

When I was starting my first business, I didn't have any money to spend on an accountant. I did my own taxes at the end of each year.

I did manage to meet several tax accountants during the planning phase. I learned that most businesspeople have a soft spot in their hearts for a starving entrepreneur. Many of them were in the same position themselves at one time.

One accountant I met knew I couldn't afford to pay him anything for his services. But he took the time to explain a few things I would need to know about doing my own taxes. He even gave me the actual IRS forms I needed to complete and advised me on things like timing, procedures, and potential audits.

That type of guidance meant a lot to a self-funded entrepreneur like me. I started working with that accountant the following year and have used his firm for over thirty years.

Choosing the right accountant is critical to your ongoing success. Make sure the chemistry between you is good and that you can envision working with him or her as a strategic advisor as well as a tax accountant.

Partner Funding

Perhaps you have decided you need help with one or more of the Four M's (Mind-Set, Marketing, Money, and Management), and you need to bring in a partner or partners to complement your abilities.

At some point, you will become unhappy with your partners (and they with you). It may be after a few months, or it may be in twenty years. But rest assured, it will happen. So only take on a partner if there is no other way to succeed. Make sure to have a written buy/sell agreement to handle the eventual split.

The question at hand is who will put up the capital to fund the new enterprise and how much equity that partner should get in the new company.

One partner may have access to capital, another may have technical expertise, another may have subject-matter expertise, another may be willing to put in more "sweat equity." How do you determine equity percentages for the various partners?

There are no formulas to provide the answer. Simply put, it's all negotiable.

Since talk is cheap, you'll likely hear a lot of puffery and BS regarding what each partner "brings to the table."

The way to deal with this situation is to reevaluate percentages annually based on the actual achievement of milestones and objectives.

For example, at one time we entered into discussions with a group of potential investors/partners who were going to "help bring PurchasingNet, Inc., to the next level." Two of the individuals didn't want to invest any of their own money but wanted an immediate majority ownership in the company.

We were willing to entertain this idea of majority ownership, but not immediately. We outlined several key milestones and tied their equity to achieving these milestones.

When presented with our thoughts, the group immediately backed off, and our discussions ended. They wanted to take over our company with no investment and no assurance of progressing to "the next level."

Take-Away #20

Talk is cheap. Build a *results-based*, dynamic model for assigning equity ownership, and reevaluate ownership percentage every year.

STAGE 1:

Preparation and Planning

Management

T he most important management task during the planning phase is figuring out what each partner will be doing and what the expectations are for each. All partners should be clear on their individual responsibilities.

It's too early to craft a mission statement or set specific goals for the organization. That will play out in the future.

Regardless of the equity percentage of each partner, there needs to be a CEO (Chief Executive Officer). This is where the buck stops. This is the tie-breaker. This is the leader.

In most cases, it will be obvious who the CEO should be. Unless your partner is your husband or wife!

Husband and Wife as Business Partners

My wife, Laurene, has been my business partner for twenty-eight years. We learned how to keep our marriage separate from our business interactions. (Mostly through trial and error!)

Many self-funded entrepreneurs work with their spouses. Our story is somewhat different from most husband-and-wife partnerships, however.

We actually cofounded PurchasingNet first and got married three years later. So we started as business partners and then became husband and wife. Most husband-and-wife business partnerships happen *after* getting married, not before.

Nonetheless, we have learned a great deal about how a husband and wife can work together effectively *and* stay married. Most people I know simply say, "I could never work with my husband [or wife]. We'd probably kill each other!"

Laurene, my business partner and wife, talking to a customer.

Here is what works for us.

First and foremost, we established roles and responsibilities at home. The responsibilities changed over the years as the needs of our daughter, Erika, changed. They weren't always split evenly, but they were clear, and there was minimal overlap.

So, for example, I was responsible for food shopping and preparing dinner Monday through Friday. When Erika was high-school age, I was responsible for taking her to school and picking her up.

Laurene was primarily responsible for Erika when our daughter was young and for doing the laundry, paying the bills, and maintaining the house. She also helped Erika with her hobbies and activities and prepared meals on the weekends.

The responsibility assignments were dynamic and negotiable, but always clear.

We agreed that using a housekeeper one day a week would be a big help (once we could afford one).

Once you have established responsibilities on the home front, you're ready to think about business roles and responsibilities.

It is important to recognize the strengths and weaknesses of each spouse, maximize the strengths, and minimize the weaknesses. It is also important to recognize you may use different styles to get things done.

Laurene and I have very different ways of doing things. That is part of the reason we make a great team. Our skill sets complement one another.

Strengths and Weaknesses

Tim	Laurene
Big-picture guy (top of the pyramid)	Strong on tasks, projects, details
Likes to get to work early and leave early	Likes to get to work late and stay late
Likes meetings and face-to-face contact with employees	Very e-mail-centric communication style
Likes to delegate as many tasks as possible	Would rather do it herself (the right way)
Good with financial data	Great taking care of clients
Looking for fast decisions and results	A perfectionist who will take her time
A bit of a slob	Meticulous
A packrat	Keeps office (and house) spotless
Strong strategically	Strong tactically

We have openly discussed our strengths and weaknesses for many hours and have tried to maximize our strengths and minimize our weaknesses. We did this by organizing the company in a way that maximized our strengths, minimized our weaknesses, and eliminated overlap so we wouldn't contradict each other—especially in front of our employees.

When we launched PurchasingNet, Laurene was responsible for sales. After a while, she gravitated toward software-implementation projects and customer service—areas she loved.

I then took the sales responsibility and became fairly good at it. I must admit, we have had many discussions over the years about who was better equipped to handle this responsibility. Eventually, we divided company responsibilities so that I was responsible for everything that took place before a sale, and Laurene took responsibility for the customer experience after the sale.

The main point here is to communicate as much as possible, maximize your individual strengths, and minimize your weaknesses. As long as you share common values and agree on your level of commitment and effort in the new business, marriage and business partnership can coexist nicely.

Legal Issues

The patent system in the United States is making some attorneys rich. It is stifling innovation and hurting small business. The system is out of control. We know this from firsthand experience testifying as a witness in a federal patent-infringement case.

As much as it pains me to say this, anyone starting a business involved in technology, invention, or innovation needs to see a patent attorney before start-up. Patent-infringement cases are simply too expensive to deal with, either as a defendant or a plaintiff.

I hope that the laws in this area will change in the near future, but the SFE should be aware of the risks before proceeding.

STAGE 2:

Launch through Breakeven

Mind-Set

> *I want one moment in time,*
> *when I'm more than I thought I could be ...*
> *When all of my dreams are a heartbeat away*
> *and the answers are all up to me.*
>
> **One Moment in Time**
> Written by Albert Hammond and John Bettis

By now, you've completed your planning and are prepared to move forward. You're ready to pull the trigger and get started!

This is the beginning of a very challenging and exhilarating stage in your entrepreneurial career. In many cases, it will take two to four years from the time you launch until the time you become cash-flow positive.

Even with all the planning and preparation, you will be faced with many, many challenges.

Fear of Failure

Many people I admire have a healthy fear of failure. The people in this category include world-class talents like Hall of Fame pro-football player Jerry Rice, legendary boxer Sugar Ray Leonard, actor Dustin Hoffman, comedian

Mike Meyers, University of Connecticut women's basketball coach Geno Auriemma, and even golf legend Arnold Palmer.

It's interesting to note that each of these folks comes from humble beginnings. They all worked very hard to overcome their shortcomings and are also very good guys!

> I was afraid to fail. The fear of failure is the engine that has driven me my entire life. The reason they never caught me from behind is because I ran scared. People always are surprised how insecure I was. The doubt, the struggles, is who I am. I wonder if I would have been as successful without them.
>
> Jerry Rice
> 2010 NFL Hall of Fame Induction
> August 7, 2010

> I was scared to lose. Just terrified of it. The first part of my career especially, the fear of doing my best and it not being good enough, of failing, was a huge motivation force for me. Jackie Burke says many great champions are basically insecure people who are secretly afraid of returning to the background they came out of, and that might have been true with me. We all love winning, but losing carried some connotations that just made it unacceptable to me. I was a gracious loser, but I sure did hate getting beat.
>
> Arnold Palmer
> *Golf Digest* (June 2007)

If you're afraid to fail, use it as a motivational tool. Besides, what's the worst thing that can happen if you do fail? Know the answer to this before proceeding.

Start-Up Traits

Some of the traits that will serve you well during this stage include versatility, flexibility, and creativity.

Versatility

One minute you can be dealing with a strategic, high level, "top of the pyramid" issue, and the next minute you'll be taking out the garbage. We have joked that it feels like you get a nosebleed from the rapid elevation changes when you run your own business.

Flexibility

Remember, the reason a business plan (the document) is overrated is because the assumptions that go into it are often wrong. As you start up your business, be ready to continually change and refine your business model.

That doesn't mean you should abandon your idea the first time you hear an objection. It does mean you need to continually reevaluate your earlier vision and assumptions as you get real-world input.

My mentor Hal Mather once told me to "make up your price in the elevator on the way up to the sales call." Somehow, you just have to trust your gut rather than a spreadsheet. The point is, don't be too rigid in your approach when launching a new enterprise. Remain open to change.

Creativity

The self-funded entrepreneur can be very creative. Creativity trumps the lack of funding every time. Here's an example.

Right after starting our software company, we had a phone conversation with the director of purchasing of a large company in Chicago called William Wrigley (the manufacturers of Wrigley's chewing gum). William Wrigley was interested in learning more about our software. They believed it would improve productivity in the purchasing department at Wrigley.

We were excited. This could be a *huge* deal for us! It would put us on the map and give us instant credibility. They sounded like they were very interested, but they wanted to come visit us at our offices before making a decision.

There was a slight problem with this. We didn't have an office! Laurene and I were working at her kitchen table in Grosse Ile, Michigan.

We desperately wanted William Wrigley to license our software, but (at that time) a billion-dollar company wouldn't spend a penny with a vendor that had no offices and was working at the kitchen table. The perceived risk would simply be too high.

So first, we needed to get an office. We couldn't afford one, but it turned out the guy who was writing the code for our software had a small office in the Renaissance Center (the "RenCen") in downtown Detroit. We asked him if we could use his conference room for a meeting and a demonstration of our software. He agreed, and we promptly made arrangements to use his facilities for the Wrigley visit.

The Wrigley executives were flying into Detroit Metro Airport. We decided that we should pick them up and drive them to the RenCen, about a half-hour ride from the airport. Laurene owned a midsize car, but we wanted to make every effort to impress our visitors. Laurene's brother had a Lincoln Town Car, and she borrowed that.

Available at Amazon.com, BN.com and other online bookstores

Web: TimMcEneny.com

Email: TimMcEneny@TimMcEneny.com

Voice: 732-768-6244

I was out of town and couldn't make the meeting (still consulting to help fund the new company). Laurene greeted our guests at the airport and promptly began to drive them to "our office."

On the way, Laurene accidentally turned on the windshield wipers while driving. Since it was a beautiful day, there was no reason to have the wipers on. Not being familiar with car, she didn't know how to turn them off! Cool under pressure, she just kept driving and talking like nothing unusual was happening.

Still somewhat rattled from the wipers, Laurene pushed on, and the adventure continued.

The RenCen is made up of four identical glass towers that are positioned at the corners of a square and are connected by long hallways. Laurene pulled into one of the parking lots and entered the RenCen, but wasn't sure where she was relative to "our office."

It turns out they had entered the RenCen just around the corner from the correct tower, but started walking in the wrong direction. After a lap around the RenCen (about a half-mile) they arrived at "our office" tower better acquainted than anticipated.

Laurene conducted the meeting, gave a killer demo, and made the executives feel comfortable with our software. The team took the shorter route back to the car and returned to the airport without incident. Wrigley called the next day and placed an order for our software. A big win! We were on our way!

A billion-dollar company just took a risk on our little company (a company with minimal revenues and no track record, but a nice office and a big car).

This story emphasizes two key points. First, the SFE (self-funded entrepreneur) must be creative, and second, the SFE must stay cool under pressure. (The SFE will be tested in many ways during all phases. Having the ability to stay calm in unusual circumstances is a tremendous asset!)

To this day, we still laugh about the Wrigley visit and what it takes to land your first big customer.

Sales Truths

I once described something I had said to a prospect as a "sales truth." It wasn't a lie, but it emphasized a positive aspect of something that was in a gray area. It was neither black nor white, but somewhere in the middle.

I define a "sales truth" as putting a positive spin on a question from a customer or prospect about a product or feature that you know (as a subject-matter expert) won't hurt the customer in any way. It's something they needn't be concerned about or fixated on.

An example might be something like this:

Question: Can your software generate "requests for quotations" from multiple vendors?

Possible Responses:
    A) Can you be more specific about your need? (An effort to change the subject.)
    B) It is limited to three at a time. (This was the case.)
    C) How often do you do that today? (Do you really need that capability?)
    D) Yes it can.

In most situations, I would opt for answer D. This assumes my knowledge of the prospect or customer is such that I know they rarely, if ever, need to generate a request for quotation to more than three vendors simultaneously.

This is an extremely important mind-set for a new SFE, particularly for people coming out of technical, quantitative, or engineering backgrounds.

What you're trying to avoid is the prospect or customer fixating on something that (in reality) is simply not that important. This can become a big issue in the customer's mind if not handled properly. Furthermore, competitors can and will try to exploit this "limitation" when selling against you.

To be clear, you must *never lie* ... but learn how to tell a "sales truth" when appropriate. It will help the prospect focus on the important considerations and will help you close business. I can honestly say that in twenty-eight years and close to 1,400 deals, we've never had a "sales truth" come back to bite us.

Underpromise and Overdeliver Rule

Don't get the impression that by telling a "sales truth," you will be shortchanging the customer. Remember, this should only be used where unimportant or irrelevant details are being questioned.

One of the most important objectives of any business is to consistently exceed customer expectations and provide a great customer experience. This is what truly matters.

Take-Away #21

When dealing with a customer, underpromise and overdeliver.

Many businesses set customer expectations very high and fall short when delivering a product or service. This is the fastest way to lose customers. It's bad business!

It is far better to set the bar lower and beat your estimates. The best compliment you can receive from a customer is that you were "on time, within budget, and exceeded expectations."

It will keep customers buying more products and services from you—and keep them away from your competitors.

Be Ready for Curveballs

No matter how much time you spent in the planning and preparation stage, you can rest assured that you missed a few important things. Don't get rattled or surprised when this happens, just fix it and move on.

One of our first customers bought steel to build clutches and brakes. When they were being educated on our products, they asked, "How does your system handle it when we buy X pounds of steel, where the price is stated in Y dollars per ton?"

Whoops! We had totally overlooked the possibility that there could be two different units of measure relating to a single purchase, so it was back to the drawing board. This was an issue that was common when ordering steel, so we had to include this capability in our software to meet the needs of the customer and the marketplace.

We let the customer know that we acknowledged our oversight and would get this feature to them as quickly as possible.

A week later, we delivered the revised software with the feature that was needed to handle the scenario. The customer ended up licensing the software and using it for many years.

Emotions: The Highs Are Higher, the Lows Are Lower

Be ready for an emotional roller coaster in the start-up phase. Compared to working for somebody else's company, life as an entrepreneur will be exhilarating one minute and devastating the next.

Managing your emotional reaction to wins and losses is important for a couple of reasons. First, it will help you maintain your sanity and keep you humble. Remember, you'll need to do something *every day* to move the business ahead, so you'll need to bounce back quickly from your setbacks. Managing emotions will help you perform more consistently.

The SFE Emotional Roller Coaster

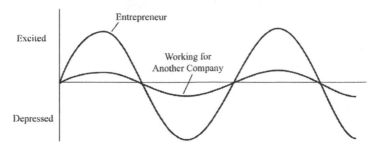

Second, your partner, employees, and even customers are easily influenced by your behavior and your reactions to the ups and downs of starting and running a business.

So even though the "highs are higher and the lows are lower," try to manage your emotions and stay on an even keel. Taking a daily break to exercise can help you deal with those emotions. It's worth the time and money to vent through physical activity. Your business may not exhibit explosive growth, but (hopefully) will be a sustainable success in the long run. Running your own business is like a marathon, not a sprint. This requires managing your emotions and behaving consistently and predictably.

The Twenty-Four Hour Rule

This simple rule saved my bacon more times than I care to remember.

There will be times when you lose your cool and get angry with someone—a customer, employee, supplier, partner.

Your inclination will be to fire back immediately and unload on the offending individual.

Don't do it!

When you feel yourself getting emotional, wait a full twenty-four hours before reacting. If at the end of the twenty-four hour cooling-off period you still feel angry, react appropriately.

Eight times out of ten, I would realize that what happened wasn't all that important, and my response would be more thoughtful and instructive. Two times out of ten, I would still be "hot" and unload accordingly.

Take-Away #22

You can't take back your words (or e-mails). Reacting emotionally simply isn't worth it.

STAGE 2:

Launch through Breakeven

Marketing

| Mind-Set | Marketing | Money | Management |

Guerrilla Marketing

"Guerilla marketing" is a concept of promoting a business that relies on time, energy, and imagination rather than a big marketing budget. It is intended to get maximum results from minimal resources. This is the recommended approach for all SFEs with limited funds for promoting their business.

The objective of guerrilla marketing is to create a unique, engaging, and thought-provoking concept that will generate buzz—and consequently turn viral. The term was coined and defined by Jay Conrad Levinson in his book *Guerrilla Marketing*. The term has since entered the popular vocabulary and marketing textbooks.

This concept calls for exploring *every* possible avenue for promoting your business, especially those requiring a small out-of-pocket investment.

The Internet fits this description perfectly. After creating your website, you can utilize SEO (search-engine optimization) techniques to help you appear at the top of the (free) search results. This is the ultimate guerilla-marketing technique. If your company or product appears in the top three search results for a given keyword or keyword phrase, you can expect hundreds or thousands of visitors clicking through to your website, all at absolutely no cost! In fact, even if you appear somewhere on the first page, you will receive many click-throughs and therefore many leads, absolutely free.

It is important to note that people are more likely to click on the top of the free search-engine listings than on the paid listings (keyword advertising).

They view the free listings as a more credible unbiased source of information than the paid listings.

Think of other avenues you can pursue at no cost or low cost. Be creative!

Here's a partial list of other ideas to consider. Some are more appropriate for consumer businesses (B2C) and others are more appropriate for products and services sold to businesses (B2B).

Technique	Comment
• Press releases	☐ Online and print media
• Fliers on cars, mailboxes, etc.	☐ Nothing fancy (one sheet okay)
• Signs	☐ Make sure you get permission to post them
• Logo on your car or car windows	☐ Becoming more popular
• Speeches and presentations	☐ You may even get paid to do these
• Trade shows (virtual or real)	☐ Can be too expensive for the SFE
• YouTube and video clips	☐ Easy to make
• Facebook	☐ Free and becoming more business-friendly
• Twitter	☐ Free and can generate website traffic
• Self-publish a booklet or book	☐ Lots of work but big potential payoff
• E-mail campaigns	☐ Low-cost and high ROI
• Host an online event	☐ Webinar, for example
• Premium items	☐ Golf balls, coffee mugs, etc.
• Write articles and blogs	☐ Online blogging and print media
• Publish case studies	☐ Great ROI

In many cases, you want to show your expertise and gain a reputation as a "domain expert" who can be called by the press and bloggers for opinions, trends, and observations.

Many people (like me) were taught at an early age not to brag or show off … especially if you were raised in the 1950s or '60s when kids were told to "be seen but not heard."

This is the time to break out of your shell! You have to promote yourself and your company. Don't think of it as bragging, just good marketing and promotion.

Others who have a tough time adjusting to the world of self-promotion are people coming from quantitative and technical backgrounds, especially those working for large companies.

In that world, self-promotion is something those "sales guys" and "headquarters people" do. Well, guess what? That's *your* responsibility now.

The difference is that big companies spend the majority of their marketing dollars on brand awareness. They spend many millions on promoting their brands with TV ads, online ads, print ads, etc.

The self-funded entrepreneur needs actionable leads, not just brand awareness. The marketing resources should be geared toward lead generation, where the emphasis is on a "call to action" and providing incentives to act now.

You want people to pick up the phone, visit your store, and click through to your website. To accomplish this, you need to write compelling copy and have a compelling reason for them to contact you *now*.

Some of the "tried and true" calls to action still work. A partial list includes:

- Discount of X Percent
- Free Estimates
- Free Gift
- Free Installation
- Additional Product
- Bonus Reward Points
- Rebates

Our Sale to Popsicle

Eight months after we launched our software company, we were running out of money. We had about $6,000 in our checking account and had accounts payable of $30,000. Our core module (Purchasing Module) had a list price of $1,995 and wasn't selling. We were surprised, because mainframe software that offered the same features and functions was selling for over $50,000. We thought that with a price this low, companies would be buying the software quickly without a long sales cycle.

Our assumption turned out to be incorrect. Regardless of the price, purchasing managers needed to get approval from top management to buy software, even if it was to be used only in purchasing. In most cases, their manager or director needed to approve the purchase of our purchasing software.

It dawned on us that people in purchasing are rewarded for getting discounts. This is how they get their "atta-boys." This is what drives and motivates a purchasing professional.

We needed a sale in the worst way, so we decided to offer a 50 percent discount for anyone who purchased our software within ninety days. We were on life support and starting to wonder if we were going to make it. We launched a direct-mail campaign to promote our special offer.

About two weeks after our mailing hit, we got a call from the purchasing manager at Popsicle (the ice-cream folks). They ordered a thirty-day trial of the software and placed an order at the end of the trial. It was only $997.50, but it kept us going a few more weeks.

Over the next couple of months, we received a flood of orders from a number of large companies. We now had some room to breathe.

We had stumbled upon a formula that we used at least once a year for the next fifteen years: the discount/deadline strategy. It was particularly successful at year-end, when companies had "available budget" and had to spend it by the end of the year or lose it the following year.

Learn what makes your prospects and customers tick, and what motivates them to actually buy your product or service. In our case, the discount/deadline proved to be a very successful call to action and was a great promotional technique.

Take-Away #23

Learn what makes your prospects and customers tick. Provide a "call to action" that will motivate them to buy your product or service *now*.

Direct Mail

Direct mail was a very effective marketing technique through the 1980s and '90s.

Direct mail can be quite expensive (compared to e-mail marketing campaigns). Costs include mail-piece design, printing, paper costs, mailing-list cost, addressing and sorting the mail piece, and postage.

It's not unusual to spend a dollar or more per piece, even for a modest direct-mail campaign.

Combine this with the fact that the response rate for a direct-mail campaign is typically less than 1 percent, and the return-on-investment analysis becomes challenging.

The math goes something like this:

Number of Pieces: 10,000 @ $1.00 each = $10,000.00

Number of Responses @ 1 percent = 100 responses

Each positive response results in a lead, so now we have 100 leads.

The lead conversion rate will vary considerably depending on the type of product or service, the quality of the piece, the call to action, the special offer, etc.

Let's say that for every ten leads you get, you can convince one of them to buy your product. This would equate to a 10 percent conversion rate, so we can forecast ten sales resulting from our mailing.

To break even, you would need to generate $1,000 in profits from each customer. Of course, you may not care if you break even, since you have just launched the business. It may be good enough to gain a few good customers who can provide referrals, references, and case studies.

Because of the high cost and the relatively low return-on-investment associated with direct mail, it is typically used for products and services that cost more than $1,000. Since 2000, direct mail has been replaced by e-mail marketing because of the low cost and relatively high return-on-investment. Nonetheless, many of the principles of direct mail can be applied to e-mail marketing campaigns.

What Do Direct Mail and E-mail Marketing Have in Common?

The single most important element is the "call to action." This type of direct marketing is *not* a good way to educate people on your product or service. It should emphasize the benefits of your offering, not how it works.

Here's where your knowledge of your market pays off. How can your product or service solve a problem that is causing the customer pain?

Break it down this way:

- Why should anyone consider your *type* of solution?
- Why consider your particular product or service?
- Why buy it now?

Identify and communicate the pain the prospect/customer is suffering. This demonstrates that you understand and want to help.

Why should the customer select you? Make sure to emphasize your unique selling proposition. What makes you the best choice? The answer might be:

- Best Value
- Superior Technology or Process
- Most Experience
- Most Customers
- Recognition from Credible Third Parties (including awards)
- References from Customers

Why should they buy now? Here's where you need a compelling offer and call to action. If they've been thinking about doing this for a while, give them a great reason to call you or visit you (or your website) now!

As for writing style, use short sentences and short paragraphs, and stay away from industry jargon and little-known acronyms. The best direct-marketing copy is written at an eighth-grade level. So keep it simple, not cluttered, and don't try to do too much educating. That can come later after you've secured the lead and qualified that lead.

You want to present only enough information to get your prospects to the next step. Presenting too much information, too soon, is counterproductive. They'll get overwhelmed, confused, and do nothing.

Think of the pyramid as a methodology for presenting information to a prospect.

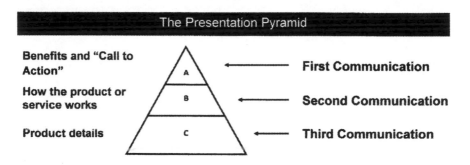

As the prospect digests and comprehends the first communication, you can proceed to the second communication where you cover the nuts and bolts of how the product works. After this communication, you can ask for the order.

Here are some of the direct-mail pieces I developed over the years.

"Hello, Purchasing Department...
Where's My Stuff?"

How to Soothe Your Savage Beast...

American Tech Inc., Colonial Commons, 670 N. Beers St., Holmdel, NJ 07733

This campaign was very successful. It struck a nerve with purchasing people. It identified their pain and let them know that we understood what they were going through. When we visited customers and prospects, many of them had this taped to their walls, monitors, and cubicles.

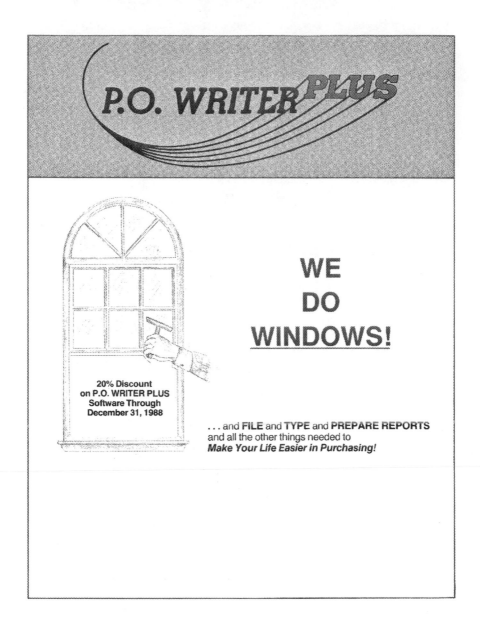

This mail piece was sent to our entire database when we launched our Windows product. It was very simple but created lots of interest (and business) based on innovative software that beat our competitors to the punch.

Purchasing Professionals... Satisfied with Your "User-Friendly" System?

"HIT ANY KEY TO CONTINUE"

It's important to make sure you capture their attention. We had lots of fun with this campaign!

The Role of the Brochure or Booklet

The importance of the printed brochure has been greatly diminished over the past few years. Websites have become the de facto brochure.

For technical or complex products, it is beneficial to have a product slick or product data sheet that lists features and functions and describes technical requirements, prerequisites, how it works, etc.

These product data sheets needn't be fancy. They should be presented to the prospect just prior to closing a deal (no sooner). It enhances your credibility in the eyes of the potential buyer and can provide the level of comfort needed to get the order.

Make sure not to provide these details too soon in the sales cycle. Doing so will only confuse and overwhelm the prospect.

Website Creation

For most businesses, a website is a necessity. The question is not whether or not you should have a website, it is who should build and maintain the website and how people can find your website.

I am a big believer in outsourcing functions that are not part of your core expertise. There are many individuals and companies who can build your website. We used Webbreez (webbreez.com) to build and host our website.

Since search-engine optimization is the most cost-effective way to get visitors to your site (it's free!), make sure that whomever you select has significant SEO experience. Do not select someone who is a graphic artist and might wind up creating a pretty website that never gets any visitors.

The key question to ask a prospective website builder is, "Do you have SEO experience, and can you provide three references where SEO helped increase the number of visitors to their website?"

As previously recommended, pick up a copy of *SEO Made Simple* by Michael Fleischner.

Free search is the first method of getting people to visit your website, and the second is paid search or keyword advertising. Google is far and away the leading search engine, so you'll want to look at the free information provided by Google on keyword-search statistics before you play this game, as it can get very expensive.

The price charged for various keywords is determined by a never-ending real-time auction. You only pay when someone clicks on your advertisement and visits one of your web pages.

The competitor who bids the highest amount appears at the top of the sponsorship list, the second-highest bidder appears second on the list, and so on. The bidders in the first three positions get the lion's share of the click-throughs. If you're listed on the right side of the Google search results page, you will receive fewer click-throughs but they will be less expensive.

One good safeguard is to establish a daily budget with Google. Once the budget is consumed, you will no longer appear as a sponsor that day.

A second safeguard is to monitor each keyword or keyword phrase you are sponsoring on a monthly basis to compare the click-through quantity to the number of visitors who are taking action. This may be defined as a visitor who fills out your request-for-information form. If you see keywords with a low-percentage conversion rate, you may want to drop them.

The third way people can arrive at your website is by clicking on a link (to your site) that is included in any document that is e-mailed or resides on any website.

The fourth way people can find your website is by keying your URL (domain name) directly into the address line of their browser. This requires people to know *and* remember your domain name and enter it in exactly as registered. This rarely happens, as it relies on people actually remembering your domain name.

Social networks like Facebook and Twitter should be used to complement your SEO and paid-search initiatives. It's free and can help generate more leads.

Case Studies and References

Case studies and references are *gold!* It is worth giving a discount or a concession in return for a case study or reference.

Of course, it will take more than a discount to have people singing your praises. People need to be thrilled with your product or service. You'll need to overdeliver to earn their case study or reference.

Prospective buyers love to see case studies and references from their areas and industries. They will feel very comfortable knowing that someone *just like them* has benefited from your product or service. They will feel like there is very little risk in doing business with you. Use a person's name, title, company, and location at the end of the case study. It adds further credibility and will result in gaining more leads and customers.

As far as the case study goes: a) get as much as you can from the customer (photos, quotes, statistics), and b) write up the case study yourself and submit it to the customer for their approval. Feel free to paraphrase the customer's thoughts to increase impact. Give them a chance to edit the case study. Even if new customers don't feel comfortable with a case study, make sure to ask them if you can use them as a reference after you know they're happy with the product or service.

Also, make sure to ask your new customers if there are any other people or companies who might be interested in buying from you. Word-of-mouth advertising is very powerful.

Our Launch: "The Demonstration Seminar"

We knew we had to educate our prospects on our software and how they could use it to increase productivity in the purchasing department. We decided to organize a three-day event we called "The P.O. Writer Demonstration Seminar."

We rented a conference room in a local Hilton hotel and scheduled five two-hour sessions per day for three straight days. We sent invitations out to all those who had expressed interest in our software and quickly filled all fifteen sessions, each devoted to one particular prospect.

Our software wasn't finished, but we had enough to demonstrate the basic features of our core module. We could work around the holes and bugs that existed at the time.

We wanted to have a user's manual completed and printed to show the attendees the supporting materials that came with the software. The user's manual was to include a self-paced tutorial that could be used to train new users.

The seminar was to begin Monday morning at 8:00 a.m. We were excited and ready to go ... or so we thought.

We found out on Friday morning that the user's manual hadn't been written. The partner who had the responsibility for writing it had waited until the last possible minute and hadn't even started to write it!

We couldn't reschedule the seminar. We had fifteen midsize to large companies ready to see our software, and we had booked the nicest hotel in town. We were committed, and there was no turning back.

I had flown into town the night before (from my consulting job). I started writing the user's manual and tutorial at 8:00 a.m. on Friday. By Sunday night at 9:00 p.m., we had a 125-page manual. Laurene and I worked our tails off and got it done, just in time!

Two interesting points about that weekend: First, it hit 100 degrees (Fahrenheit) in Detroit that weekend ... an all-time record. We didn't have an office (keeping the overhead low), so we worked at Laurene's house in Grosse Ile, Michigan. Although it was a nice little ranch house, it didn't have air conditioning. It was so hot and humid that the pages of the user's manual were sticking together. It was a little stressful, but we worked through it and made the deadline.

Take-Away #24

When you're an SFE, you "will it to happen." Failure is not an option.

The second interesting point from that weekend is that the tutorial we wrote as we were racing against the clock was used virtually unchanged by thousands of people over the next fifteen years. Sometimes you do your best work when you're under tremendous pressure.

It's something like the "Busy Bartender Syndrome." Have you ever noticed that the service at most bars is better when it's crowded and the bartenders are running at top speed? Conversely, when there are just a few people at the bar, it takes quite a while to get served.

The demonstration seminar came off quite well. In fact, we got our very first order—from a small company in Ann Arbor, Michigan, named Flo-Ezy Filters.

They had two people attending a two-hour session: one gray-haired gentleman dressed in a three-piece suit and one young guy in Army camouflage gear. We naturally assumed the man in the three-piece suit was "the boss." Turns out that was a bad assumption. The young guy was the owner of the company, and the guy in the three-piece suit was his purchasing manager!

Take-Away #25

Always get the titles of the prospects and gain an understanding of how, and by whom, the final decision will be made. Don't make any assumptions.

The purchasing manager was very concerned about doing business with a start-up. Laurene explained that we were running the business from her home; she offered her address and phone number, and she asked if he would feel better with her Social Security number as well (this was long before identity theft had become an issue). They developed an instant rapport. Years later, Del and his wife would attend our wedding.

Take-Away #26

Be a "straight shooter." Purchasing managers are hired to manage risk and know when to take a chance on a new firm or technology.

We got the order, ended up getting a great customer (who would end up helping us create a better product), and got tons of good input from all the attendees of the demo seminar. It was even better than a focus group (used to get opinions about a product or service). The input was from real prospects looking at a real product.

They were looking at the real product and giving us their honest reaction to it. We also started to learn that spending two hours on a product demonstration as Step 1 was not the best way to sell. It was too much, too soon. They were starting to glaze over and were overwhelmed after thirty minutes. It would have been much more powerful to talk about the benefits of using the product and discussing case studies. The problem was we didn't have any. All we had was the product.

Sales versus Marketing

Think of marketing as one-to-many selling and sales as being comprised of one-to-one activities that culminate in an order.

Marketing is fun, but difficult to measure. Selling is a lot of hard work and very easy to measure.

Anyone who thinks sales is an easy job designed for slackers has never done it before. Sales requires incredible self-discipline and tremendous self-motivation. In my opinion, sales is the most difficult job in any company. You need to be willing to withstand constant rejection and experience only occasional victories.

Sales is a numbers game. For every ten leads, you might only close one of them. Think of a funnel:

Leads flow into the funnel at a far faster rate than orders come out.

Leads can come from various marketing programs (including your website and outbound telemarketing). Once the leads have been generated, they need to flow through a sales process that hopefully results in an order.

Outbound telemarketing is arduous work. Most people like doing it about as much as getting a root canal. New stockbrokers begin their careers by making 250 outbound phone calls a day to people whose names appear on a list or in a directory. They are given a script and a phone, and they start "dialing for dollars."

These cold calls are difficult to make but can yield fruit if you have patience and a thick skin. You can't take rejection personally.

A much higher-percentage telemarketing activity is to only call those who have already expressed interest in your product or service. Perhaps they filled out a form on your website or called for information. These are warm leads and may be ready to take the next step.

Leads

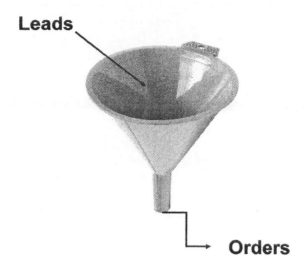

Orders

What Is the Next Step?

When you first start up your business, you have no idea how a lead will turn into a sale. You need to define and continually refine your sales process as you get more sales cycles under your belt.

The first step in most sales processes is to qualify the lead. Do they possess the attributes of a likely customer? This might mean having enough income, assets, budget, pain, motivation, knowledge, infrastructure, etc. In other words, are they capable of actually buying your product or service? Do they have the minimum prerequisites to become a customer? The sales-funnel breakdown might look something like this:

Prospect List	5,000 Names
Expressed Some Interest	200 Suspects
Qualified Prospects	100 Prospects

Lead Qualification

Some of the things you'll hear from suspects who are clearly not qualified prospects:

1. "I have no money to spend."
2. "I have no budget."

3. "You must follow our sales process if you want to win our business, including submitting a response to an RFI (request for information) followed by an RFP (request for proposal) and conducting multiple onsite meetings." This process is often too expensive and will eat up all the profits before you ever get an order.
4. "I am unemployed and would like to come to work for your company."
5. "I'm trying to collect information to write my master's thesis."
6. An assortment of other bizarre stories, including being an inmate in federal prison or being in Central Africa with no Internet connectivity.

Once these have been eliminated from your list of suspects, you can focus your time and energy on good, winnable business.

Sales Process

The remaining steps in the sales process depend on the length of your sales cycle (ours was six to twelve months) and the particulars of your industry and competitors.

In general, there are certain principles that should be followed.

1. Make it easy for the customer to do business with you (no complicated price lists or order forms).
2. Avoid high-pressure sales tactics. Think of yourself as an enabler, educator, and consultant. You can't sell something to someone who doesn't want to buy. You can only sell to someone who wants to buy—and you can make it a faster, smoother sales cycle that will get the customer off to a good start.
3. Educate, educate, educate. The prospect needs to learn what to expect from your company and your product or service. Client expectations can only be set through education. This is ultimately what will make for a satisfied customer.

We used a technique called "drip marketing" to educate prospects during the sales cycle. Every thirty days, we would send an e-mail that was educational and usually profiled a customer's experience with our product and service. Since you may not have many reference-able customers, you can quote industry statistics or industry analysts who are respected in your field.

This "adds value" in the sales cycle and helps differentiate you from your competitors. It is not just sales-oriented information; it concentrates on actual return-on-investment, benefits, and implementation experiences. Using an e-mail approach to education is a very cost-effective way to communicate with and educate your prospects. Another method we used extensively was conducting online seminars or "webinars." (More on this topic later.)

Closing the Deal

As the sale progresses, you will start to get positive buying signals from your prospects. This might be the prospect saying "When we implement it we will ..." or "We could be flexible when we implement your product," or also "Once we start using your product."

When prospects get really serious about buying your product or service, they typically start to get a little scared and nervous. They want to make sure they're getting the best possible deal and that there are minimal risks.

So if you've been progressing through the sales cycle and all of a sudden the prospect gets a little goofy, that isn't necessarily a bad thing. In fact, it shows you are "coming down the home stretch" and are entering the final phase of the sales cycle.

They will then proceed to "squeeze you" to get a better price and start asking for references. Stay cool, even if you really need the sale.

At this point, it might be a good idea to ask the prospect what kind of price they had budgeted for. If it is a reasonable offer, consider accepting their offer (provided they place their order no later than X date and agree to be a reference or case study).

Take-Away #27

If you act like you really need a sale, you'll never get it. Prospects are like children and dogs ... they can tell when you're scared.

You could also respond with something like, "I can't meet your price expectation, but I can give you [a concession like free training, free delivery, free installation]." In these cases, it's best to give something that has value to the customer but costs you very little in out-of-pocket expenses.

At this point in the company's history, it's always best to be "on the side of the deal" and get the order sooner rather than later.

As far as reference requests, if you don't have any, consider offering a money-back guarantee or "final payment upon satisfaction." This may be necessary to ease the prospect's fear and minimize the perceived risk in working with you.

Don't be afraid to "leave some money on the table" during your first negotiations. Consider the lifetime revenue that will be derived from the customer relationship. The important thing is to get the order and get on with it.

STAGE 2:

Launch through Breakeven
Money

Through the start-up period, cash-flow management is critical to survival. Cash is the lifeblood of any company. Running out of cash in the early stages of development is like being on life support.

Controlling cash flow is easy to understand but difficult to do. There are only two ways the SFE can manage cash flow: first, by maximizing sales revenues, and second, by minimizing costs. If you are successful in these two areas, you will become profitable and thrive. If you aren't, you may not survive.

The companies that are backed by venture capital or third-party funding (less than 1 percent of all companies) don't have the same pressures to manage cash. They can always make another "trip to the well" for a cash infusion. Assuming those companies are showing some progress, they can get more cash.

The same is not always true for the self-funded entrepreneur. You don't want to have to take out a second mortgage or home-equity loan if you don't have to.

Maximizing Sales Revenues

During the start-up stage, it is very difficult to get every penny out of every sale. The objective is to get as many customers onboard as quickly as possible. This requires discounts and concessions to ensure you can build your customer base as quickly as possible.

But there's one thing in particular you can do to get to the break-even point as quickly as possible: include an ongoing maintenance program as part of your product or service offering. This will create recurring revenue that will improve your cash flow and increase the value of your business.

Integrate this program in your sales and marketing efforts. Don't treat it like the "extended warranty" that electronics and appliance retailers offer as they are ringing up the sale. These are perceived to have little value, and most savvy shoppers decline them.

Make sure your ongoing maintenance program offers real value to the customer. Make it part of your selling process, and use it to differentiate your offering from those of your competitors.

When we started our software business, we licensed (sold) our software to companies and then provided support and maintenance on an hourly basis. We billed in six-minute increments (.1 hour). Two years after our launch, we realized we were missing a big opportunity. We started to offer a client support program (CSP) to our customers. It included many benefits for one annual fee. The CSP offering included unlimited phone support and discounts on future purchases. All new releases of the software were free to customers participating in the program.

The good news for us is that we could charge 33 percent of the upfront purchase price every year the customer was in the program. The only way we would lower this percentage was if the customer committed to a multiyear agreement (two, three, or five years).

Within one year of introducing this program, we hit our break-even point. We were profitable from that point forward.

It should be noted that another software company had a program very similar to this, and we simply replicated their program in our environment. Don't be afraid to copy concepts that work.

Maintenance may not be applicable for every business, but recurring revenue is a concept that applies to most successful businesses. Think of any way possible to generate revenue (cash) on an ongoing basis with every customer. For example, even if you own a restaurant or a dry-cleaning store, you can implement a program to encourage future visits and purchases. I had dinner at a seafood restaurant recently that gave us a "Fish Bucks" card that was something like a frequent-flyer program. It entitled us to get discounts on future meals. The meal was very good, and their "Fish Bucks" card provided an incentive to return.

In summary, a plan to generate recurring revenue is a key to success for the SFE's business. I can honestly say that without our CSP offerings, we never would have turned the corner and generated positive cash flow.

> ## Take-Away #28
>
> If you see a successful program being used by another company (in any industry), don't be afraid to adopt it. There is no need to reinvent the wheel.

Minimizing Costs

On the other side of the equation are the costs of running the business. Using the SFE Sink Analogy, think of water draining out of the sink as cash leaving your bank account. These are the expenses needed to launch and run the business.

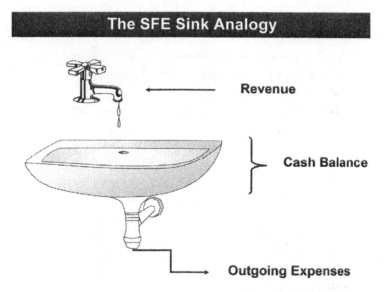

The SFE Sink Analogy

Revenue

Cash Balance

Outgoing Expenses

First, your versatility will be critical to minimizing costs. Part of what allows SFEs to unlock their entrepreneurial potential is surviving the first few years of the new enterprise. This can only be done by you (and your partners) wearing many hats and doing as much as possible yourself. Of course, you'll want to pay yourself the bare minimum (if anything at all) until you start approaching the break-even point.

Second, consider outsourcing and/or partnering with other individuals or firms to provide services necessary to launch your company.

When launching our software company, we actually outsourced software development to a company who saw potential in our idea and was willing to do the programming for a 10 percent royalty fee. The other company ended up recouping its "investment" and made a decent profit. We ended up conserving cash and only paid them the royalty thirty days after we actually received cash from the customer.

Third, negotiate with all of your suppliers to get lower prices and better payment terms. You will find a number of suppliers and service providers have a soft spot in their hearts for the SFE. Perhaps they started the same way you did, and they understand the limitations on your funds and your need to conserve cash.

Here are ten SFE negotiating tactics you may find useful when negotiating with suppliers:

1. Ask if they have some flexibility on their price and payment terms. Remember the old saying, "If you don't ask, you don't get."

2. Let a supplier know you intend to use them exclusively if they can meet your needs. Share your long-term vision with them and indicate they can receive more business from you in the future.

3. Ask them to match the lowest price you've been quoted (or know of) for the same or similar products or services.

4. Tell your supplier you only have a budget of X for this project, and if they can meet that price you can commit immediately.

5. Tell your supplier you've gotten approval from your board (or your partners) to spend X on this project. If you want to spend more, you will have to go back for their approval, and you don't know how long it will take.

6. Enter into a longer-term agreement in exchange for lower prices early in the agreement.

7. Agree to pay cash in return for a substantial discount.

8. Ask for payment terms that stretch over months. If not, ask for ninety-day payment terms. If not, consider a credit card with cash-back rebates or rewards points.

9. Get better pricing or receive referral fees (cash or credits) by referring business to them.

10. Explore barter deals where you can provide your products or services in return for their products or services with no cash exchanging hands.

As an SFE, you'll be too busy to get three quotes from different suppliers for each good or service you will need to launch your company. This is the practice of larger public companies and government agencies that have purchasing or procurement professionals on staff. You simply don't have time to do this, so utilize one or more of the ten SFE negotiating tactics to reduce expenses and stop water (cash) from going down the drain.

STAGE 2:

Launch through Breakeven

Management

Hiring

Ideally, you'll be in a position to hire one or more people a few months after the launch. Almost all successful entrepreneurs will tell you that the secret to their success is hiring (and retaining) great people. I would agree—there's nothing more important than hiring the right people. People do make the difference.

Here are fifteen principles for hiring great people:

1. Pay your new hire as much as you can possibly afford. You want to hire the best possible people. Think of this as an investment in your business, not an expense. Regardless of the type of business you start, the quality of the people you hire will ultimately determine your success or failure.

2. Don't be afraid to hire people who are smarter than you. You'll need to get as many smart people as you can to help you survive and thrive. Don't be insecure. Check your ego at the door before (and after) you hire.

3. Never use "head hunters." They're too expensive, and you can do better by simply running help-wanted ads online and in the Sunday newspaper.

4. Use telephone interviews extensively before inviting a candidate to visit with you in person. It saves time and eliminates the weak candidates quickly.

5. Sometimes you'll want to hire someone based on his or her unexpected availability to you (read laid off). We did this many times when a good customer of ours became available.
   Note: *Never talk to or hire an employee of a current customer if he or she is still employed. It's bad for business.*
   Sometimes you should hire great people based on their availability, not yours. It may cost a little bit more, but it's worth it to get great people.

6. Try to conduct your onsite interview like a conversation, not an interrogation. Put the candidate at ease by talking briefly about your company and your plans for the future. Move on to a few "softball questions" before getting to more meaningful discussions.

7. No matter how bad the candidate may be:

   a. Be nice.

   b. Try to learn something (about anything) as a result of the interview. It shouldn't be a total waste of time.

8. Ask about the candidate's success and failures, strengths and weaknesses, and what they learned from previous jobs. Wait until the candidate relaxes before asking your tougher questions.

9. Avoid silly interview questions like, "Where do you want to be five years from now?" No one knows this. Visibility today rarely exceeds one year.

10. Check references—both the ones that are given by the candidate and those that aren't given. My favorite question to a reference was, "Assuming you subscribe to the theory that everyone has weaknesses, what would you say his/hers are?" If that reference can't come up with at least one weakness, ignore everything else he or she said. This information can also help you manage employees if they do come onboard.

11. Do a background check before making an offer. You might have to pay a small fee, but it can help you prevent a bad hire. Check for more than traffic violations. Include a search for criminal record, financial condition, degrees, and citizenship status.

12. For lower-level positions, make the offer subject to your review after a ninety-day trial period. This will give you a chance to see how the candidate performs and to check their reliability, flexibility, etc. We hired a lady for a clerical position in our young company. We immediately noticed that our accounts receivables dropped quite a bit after we hired her. One of her responsibilities was to prepare invoices to send to a customer after a new sale. Unfortunately, when she got behind in her work, she would put partially completed invoices in her brown paper lunch bag and stuff it in her desk. Sad but true. (You can't make this stuff up!) It was time for her to move on.

13. Look for people who can become part of a team—your team. People who have backgrounds in the military, team sports, or bartending typically are good team players.

14. Don't be afraid to hire someone who has some weaknesses. We hired many "corporate misfits" over the years who were fantastic employees, but didn't fit the corporate mold.

15. Not every new hire works out. If you make a bad hire you'll usually know within ninety days. Cut your losses quickly and move on!

   Reasons to be cautious:
   - The "Swiss cheese" resume—lots of job-changing is a red flag.
   - Switching industries—if someone has spent a long time in one industry, it may be difficult to transition.
   - Experience only with large companies—may not be able to adjust to working in a small company.
   - Late to the interview—probably not reliable.
   - Resume inaccuracies—dates of employment and educational degrees should be verified.
   You should disqualify any candidate with these issues.

Once the New Hire Is Onboard

The length of the learning curve for a new hire varies depending on the job. For a clerical position, you can usually tell if you have made a good hire within thirty days. For a salesperson, it might take six to twelve months before you see results.

If you suspect that you might have made a mistake and that the new employee will fall short of expectations, you owe it to him or her (and yourself) to:

- Identify the specific issue(s)
- Provide the necessary training
- Monitor progress
- Communicate frequently with the employee
- Develop an action plan to improve performance
- Document the above (you will need it if a complaint is filed later on)

If you determine the employee can't meet expectations, cut him or her loose ASAP ... but only after going through each of the steps outlined.

I made several costly mistakes during the history of our software company. Two of these mistakes were people that I had worked with at another company. They were both solid performers at that company (a large manufacturing company), but they simply couldn't make the transition to a small software company. I never should have hired them in the first place. I tried and tried to help them make it, but they just never "got it."

One was a high-level manager with a nice six-figure compensation package. I invested two years in him before we pulled the plug. Great guy, but not a good fit. He was too accustomed to the "big company" ways (large staffs, lots of meetings, etc.). Not only was this hire a very expensive mistake, but it also hurt company morale, slowed our growth, and consumed too much of my time.

Bad hires are one of the biggest and most costly mistakes the SFE can make. So take your time and get it right! You'll never have a 100 percent success rate, but a 75 percent "good hire" rate is a reasonable goal.

How Much to Pay New Hires

You'll want to be competitive with other companies in your area, so check online for statistics of wages paid in your area by job title. If you're not competitive, expect high turnover—a very disruptive force. When the market conditions favor the employee's negotiating position, and he or she wants more money than you can afford to pay, here are some tips for how to hire for less while still keeping employees motivated:

- Pay a low base salary with periodic performance bonuses (or commissions) based on actual achievements.

- Start their salary low, but promise a performance/salary review in six to twelve months. If they're as good as they think, they will be able to demonstrate their abilities within this time period and get a raise to meet their expectations.

- Pay a low salary but promise stock options (or some other incentive) with vesting over five years. This usually only applies to management positions or key employees.

- Hire temporary workers as contractors whenever possible and have them pay their own benefits. Each year you fill out a 1099 form with the pay they received from you. This will also save you the Social Security tax you would normally pay if they were a full-time employee. Before using this approach, check with your advisors to make sure you're not in violation of any tax or workers' compensation laws.

- Hire someone as an intern (paid or unpaid) with the opportunity to become a full-time employee.

Make sure to see if you are eligible for any tax breaks if and when you hire. This can soften the cash-flow impact of hiring a new person.

Remember to look at outsourcing and/or bartering if you can save money and improve cash flow. You can even outsource bookkeeping, accounting, telemarketing, and almost anything else you can imagine. As long as it's not a core competency of your company, consider outsourcing it.

Time Management

This stage of the business cycle requires tremendous focus and dedication. The SFE is trying to do all the things necessary to make it to the break-even point while also doing things that will help meet long-term objectives.

The SFE's Time-Management Pyramid can be used to help manage your time. Some people call this Pareto's Law or the 80-20 Rule. This technique helps separate the "vital few" from the "trivial many."

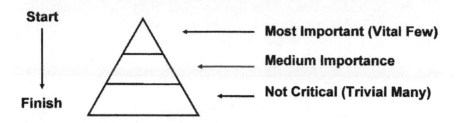

The first step in this process is to create a to-do list for everything you want to accomplish in a given day or week. Next, place an A, B, or C next to each of the tasks.

Start off your day by doing a couple of the easy C tasks and cross them off the list. This gets you in the positive frame of mind and ready to tackle the more important tasks.

Try to complete at least one A and one B task every day. Use the C tasks as filler. Keep your to-do list in front of you all day long, and you will be amazed how much you can get done. Encourage your employees to do the same.

Add new tasks to the bottom of your to-do list as the day progresses. At the end of the day, develop a new to-do list for tomorrow. This will allow you to think about what you have to do the next day (maybe you'll even dream about it!). When you start the new day, you'll be focused and ready to go.

Take Notes!

There's nothing more aggravating than people in business who don't take notes and then forget what they're supposed to do. Some try to work from memory but invariably forget one or two important tasks. The second most frustrating thing is people who do take notes and then lose them (or can't find them).

Do yourself and everyone else a favor and take notes on a laptop (or equivalent) or in a spiral notebook. At the end of the every day or week, go through your notes and incorporate open items into your to-do list.

Policies and Procedures

As a general rule, policies-and-procedures manuals aren't worth the paper they're written on. They discourage independent thinking and common sense.

You want people to think "outside the box" and do whatever is necessary to get the job done.

Formal policies and procedures are typically a crutch for weak managers. When you make it to the break-even point, you can develop some guidelines (not policies) for business hours, vacations, and sick time. In the meantime, the focus needs to be on doing whatever is necessary for the business to survive and make it to Stage 3: Achieving and Maintaining Profitability.

STAGE 3:

Achieving and Maintaining Profitability
Mind-Set

> *I've been taking care of business, it's all mine.*
> *Taking care of business and working overtime.*
>
> **Takin' Care of Business**
> Written by Randy Bachman

Reaching the Break-Even Point

If you've made it to the point where your sales revenues exceed your expenses, you've passed the break-even point! You are now "cash-flow positive." This is truly a great achievement and a cause for celebration, but not for too long—there is still lots of work to do!

Many entrepreneurs reach the break-even point but have difficulty maintaining profitability over the long haul.

During the start-up phase, you put it all on the line and work nonstop to achieve profitability. It's fun, challenging, and exhausting all at the same time.

You now have an opportunity to shift gears and think of this stage as the beginning of a marathon. That doesn't mean you're now on Easy Street. It is an opportunity, however, to establish some balance in your life.

The beauty of being an SFE (self-funded entrepreneur) is that you can set your own priorities and objectives. My definition of success is building a great, vibrant business and having a great, loving family at the same time.

81

These were (and are) my priorities. Not all entrepreneurs feel the same way. I've heard entrepreneurs say things like, "We're going to go public or die trying." Their sole purpose for existing is their business. Many ignore their spouses while running their businesses, and their marriages crumble. Others work themselves into an early grave. Others turn to alcohol and drugs. The pressure is enormous … if you let it get to you.

My personal definition of success is "to live a balanced life." SFEs have a great opportunity to create this life for themselves and their families, and now is the time to start. This balance will also keep you from burning out too soon.

Money shouldn't be *the* driving force for an entrepreneur. But you should make money while you can. Remember that as an SFE, you'll need to pay yourself a reasonable salary (and bonus), finance the operation and growth of the company, and pay for your own retirement someday. There is a finite amount of time to make money, so don't be afraid to make a good profit whenever you can. Profit is not a dirty word!

The objective at Stage 3 should be to build an infrastructure and team to ensure:

- a) You make a profit every year.
- b) You've built a strong enough foundation to support future growth.
- c) You can take time off when needed.

After you've struggled through the start-up and break-even phases, it feels a bit surreal to be receiving money that you're not sure what to do with. Do you spend it? Do you save it? Do you invest it in the stock market? Do you reinvest it in the company?

I remember getting about $600 per month in interest from a local bank (interest rates were about 9 percent back then.) I was meeting our monthly personal expense with the salary I was drawing from the business—this was truly "extra money." I looked at my monthly bank statement and thought I had died and gone to heaven—it was a great feeling. After starting penniless, this was a new sensation, and I liked how it felt.

Friends

As someone once said, "If you own your own business and you want a friend, buy a dog." Between the business and your personal and family life, you're lucky if you can maintain your old friendships and relationships.

Although you can socialize a bit with your employees, you can't get too close to them. The reason is simple. There may be times when you have to make tough decisions regarding your employees. For example, if you are very friendly with an employee and you have to promote someone, and you choose your friend, the rest of the employees will be upset because you promoted someone "just because they were your friend." It can hurt morale. Conversely, if you don't promote the friend, you risk damaging the friendship. Either way, you lose. It is best to keep your relationships with your employees strictly professional.

As you become successful, some of your "friends" will become jealous and resentful. Not everyone will be happy for your success. But if you're struggling, these same people are happy. Misery must love company. Don't be surprised or discouraged when this happens to you—and it certainly will.

Invest in Your Own Company

You'll never get a better return-on-investment than when you invest (or reinvest) in your own company. If you're torn between investing in your company or someone else's (stock market), pick yours every time. Since you are now generating free cash flow, reinvest at least part of it to build your infrastructure and your organization. Save the rest for a rainy day and live *below* your means.

We've all heard at least one story of an entrepreneur who drove his leased luxury car to the proverbial poorhouse. Fight the urge to demonstrate your success too soon. Having a cash cushion will buy you the good night's sleep that many overextended entrepreneurs wish they had.

What Lies Ahead

After reinvesting some of the profits to build your infrastructure and team, you'll want to be in a position to grow the company (if you so choose). Some SFEs would opt for no growth or slow growth based on the life balance they have chosen. *That's okay!* There's nothing wrong with working solo and (just) making a good living.

This is not an option for companies funded by institutional investors. They have to try to achieve "hypergrowth" so their investors can cash out through an IPO or M&A transaction (mergers and acquisitions). The SFE is in it for the long haul and can control his or her own destiny.

Start thinking about how much growth you want to experience. That will help determine the type and amount of reinvestment you will need to make. Your plans may include a new office, more employees, hardware, and software. This planning will also determine the kind of organization you want to build and the type of people you will want on your team (e.g. those with experience growing a company).

Lifetime Learning

Just because you've reached profitability doesn't mean you can stop reading and learning. I tried to spend at least two hours a day reading and numerous hours a day learning throughout the twenty-eight-year history of our software company. That commitment to learning continues to this day.

This is a critical part of successfully running your company and managing change. You have to know what the rest of the world is doing to improve productivity, performance, and profitability in order to continually improve the performance of your company.

One way to do this is to have a formal (or informal) board of advisors to help you become aware of new trends and techniques. It will also provide a sounding board for your ideas.

There's no substitute for reading, either online or print. I read ten to fifteen weekly or monthly publications on a regular basis, most covering business and technology. I never read them cover to cover (not enough time) but skimmed them to get a sense of what was happening around me.

Take-Away #29

It's what you learn after you know it all that counts.

—John Wooden
Legendary Basketball Coach

Have Fun!

It's okay to have some fun in business.

One sale we made was to the Trump Organization in New York City. I was dealing with an old-timer I'll call Harvey. He had worked for "The Donald" for quite a while and was very loyal to him. Harvey was pushing me for a big discount on our software, and I didn't want to give him one.

After going back and forth for a few minutes, I said to him that I would play Mr. Trump in golf, and if he beat me, I would give him the software for free. If I beat him, Harvey would pay full price. Thank goodness our golf match never happened. I found out later that Donald usually shot in the 70s and I shot in the mid- to high 80s. I would have lost about $100,000 on that match!

I ended up making the sale (giving a small discount), and Mr. Trump autographed one of his books for me. We all had a laugh, and it helped pave the way for a good business relationship.

A Merger or Acquisition on the Horizon?

Believe it or not, now is the time to start thinking about selling your business. It's probably too soon to sell it now—you'll want to enjoy the many benefits of owning a successful enterprise.

You will want to start factoring into your thought process what a potential acquirer might be looking for in a company. So for example, if you are in the software business, the development platform (programming language) you choose could attract or turn off a potential acquirer.

We migrated from an old programming language that became obsolete to a newer, web-based Microsoft development platform that was and is very popular with software developers worldwide. This made us more interesting to potential acquirers that used similar development methodologies.

I might add that this isn't to say it was the easiest, fastest, most reliable development platform, but it was one of the two most popular platforms (Java was the other), and so it made us more of a mainstream company.

Some of the other things potential acquirers look for are GAAP (generally accepted accounting principles) accounting systems instead of cash-basis accounting. In a cash-basis account system, you recognize revenue only when you receive payment and expenses only when you actually spend money.

Don't obsess over these acquisition-oriented considerations, just start thinking about them. It's more important that you continue to satisfy customers and maintain profitability.

STAGE 3:

Achieving and Maintaining Profitability
Marketing

| Mind-Set | Marketing | Money | Management |

Sales Approach

Hopefully you have a strong flow of leads coming into your "funnel." Now is the time to formalize the process of converting leads into sales.

Up to this point, you've been doing whatever's needed to get the deal, and you've probably been doing it all yourself. Before running out and hiring a sales rep, you should be able to answer the question, "Do I want to sell direct or through third parties, or both?"

Generally speaking, more complex products and services fit the direct-sales model. Simple, more easily understood products are candidates for third-party resellers.

More complex products require in-depth knowledge and lots of training for the salesperson. These folks are best kept under your control as dedicated sales reps selling only your products. It will allow them to properly focus their energies and build their product knowledge.

It is obviously more expensive to build a dedicated sales force—you're absorbing 100 percent of their compensation, training, traveling, and learning-curve costs. But you're controlling their sales process, their focus, and their dedication to you and your company.

The other approach is to recruit distributors, OEMs (original equipment manufacturers), resellers, or franchises to sell your product. If your product is a commodity or a well-known product that is understood by the marketplace, you might consider the third-party approach. It is less costly than direct selling, but there is also less control of resellers and how much attention they give to your business. They tend to sell whatever they can sell quickly and easily with the highest return-on-investment.

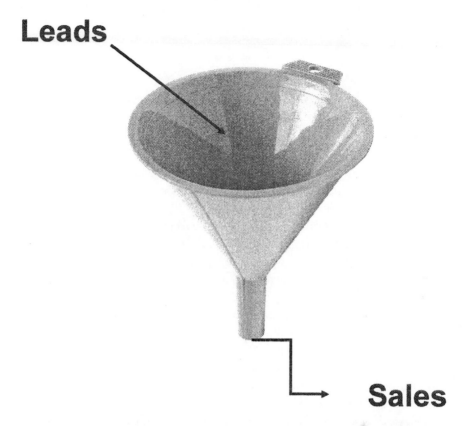

During the twenty-eight-year history of our software company, we attempted to use eleven different resellers for our procurement software. Only one was successful; the others fell short of expectations. Not only did they sell very little (if anything at all), but we also spent countless hours educating and training them on how our product worked and how to sell it.

Our software was easy to use but hard to sell. It required an in-depth knowledge of the business processes associated with procurement through accounts payable. It was a complex sale.

We tried and tried to make the resellers successful, but it never worked. We concluded that the best way for us to work with third parties was on a referral basis. Anything they referred to us that we closed resulted in a 10 percent referral fee.

This model worked best. We could refer business to them, and they could refer business to us. It worked quite well and cost very little to maintain. We simply sent out a monthly e-mail to all the third parties who referred business to us in order to keep them up-to-date on new customers, success stories, and software enhancements. It kept them "pumped up" and knowledgeable. It worked well and was truly a win-win situation.

Telesales versus Sales Calls

It has been said that the cost of making an in-person sales call is somewhere between $250 and $1,000, depending on the mode of transportation and time involved. Personally, I think it could be even higher than $1,000.

Fortunately, there are many tools available on the web that reduce the need to make a sales call. These include conference-calling services, GoToMeeting and WebEx (to share presentations and demonstrations in real time), and Skype (for video conference calls).

We took advantage of all of these tools to reduce the number of in-person sales calls. If, however, your competition is making in-person sales calls, you will end up doing the same. All you need to hear from a prospect is that "competitor X" made a sales call, and it leaves you little choice but to visit them.

For lower-priced products and services, telesales is just fine—especially if your competitors aren't making in-person calls. It costs far less and can be just as effective. The most productive telephone calls are to follow up on warm leads. You can qualify the lead, begin to develop a relationship, and move through the sales cycle without physically visiting the prospect—if you use the online tools effectively.

We made numerous six-figure sales without a single in-person sales call.

Webinars

We conducted twenty-four webinars per year. The out-of-pocket costs were minimal, and the results were extraordinary. We conducted twelve "Introduction to PurchasingNet" webinars and twelve "Best Practice" webinars every year.

The "Introduction to PurchasingNet" webinar lasted about forty-five minutes; it was educational and a very soft-sell of our software. It reduced our cost of selling, because we would get ten to twenty companies to attend every month, and this would eliminate the need for an individual introductory software demonstration. We would allow anyone (except competitors) to attend these webinars because our incremental cost of adding another attendee was zero.

It was a great way to start a sales cycle. It gave us instant credibility and was a way for us to demonstrate our domain expertise. We could also record the webinar and make it available on the WebEx website for a small additional cost.

The "Best Practice" webinars featured a customer or referral partner, their case study, and more in-depth information on a particular topic. These sessions were very well-attended (sometimes up to a hundred people) and built our knowledge of the needs of our marketplace.

To increase attendance, we sent a short e-mail to all of the customers and prospects in our CRM system (customer relationship management). The cost of this type of e-mail blast was minimal. The e-mail included links to our website.

The people attending registered on the website. The webinar was conducted through WebEx, an Internet service that we subscribed to that had a very reasonable monthly fee.

In summary, this is a very cost-effective way to sell, ideal for almost any SFE. To learn more about Internet services that can be used to conduct webinars, see *www.webex.com* and *www.gotomeeting.com*.

Sales Methodologies

There are numerous ways to sell. We used the "solution selling" methodology, which was particularly effective in selling software and services to midsize and large companies.

The methodology defines a process for selling based on various principles and techniques, such as gaining access to power. This enables the salesperson to deal with the ultimate decision-maker during the sales cycle. This methodology was designed primarily for selling complex solutions to large corporations and institutions.

There are many different methodologies for different industries and different types of businesses. Even if you are selling to the public, you should establish or select a methodology that's right for you—or create your own so you can train your salespeople and keep everyone on the same page. Pretty much everyone agrees that fast-talking, high-pressure sales tactics are a thing of the past and don't work well in any type of business.

The principle of "consultative selling" is widely accepted as a more effective approach. Here the salesperson is working with prospects to help them define their requirements and to provide an appropriate product or service to help them meet their needs. It requires a little more time and patience, but often yields better results.

It is important in sales to listen more than you speak. The consultative selling approach begins with asking lots of relevant questions. This demonstrates your desire to help the prospect while giving you insight into the true needs of the prospect. You can then build your own credibility and strategically approach each sales opportunity. Most likely, there will be some prospect education to accomplish before you can move to the next step in the sales process.

Take-Away #30

A consultative salesperson is one who can resist the temptation to "pitch" their product or service until they have laid a solid foundation for future selling.
(Source: *www.sales-sense.com*)

Think about what happens when you visit a doctor. Before prescribing a solution to your problem, a doctor must first examine you, talk to you, and analyze test results. The sales process is very similar. You wouldn't be too happy if the doctor started writing a prescription before looking at you. You would immediately question his or her competence.

Take-Away #31

In sales, analyze before your prescribe a solution. Listen more than you speak.

Recon

Some business leaders believe you should only think about your own company and not worry about the competition. Clearly, they are not SFEs.

I would argue that even if you are the "Best in Class" company, you need to pay attention to the competition. Competitors can help make your company better, no matter how big or small you may be.

I visited the website of each of our top five competitors at least once a month. I always had someone (other than me) register on the websites so we would receive their e-newsletters, press releases, webinar invitations, etc.

We wanted to learn as much as we could about the competitors' products, pricing, promotion, and position. We read new press releases and looked for any organizational changes that had taken place. Knowing who the new managers were was helpful in predicting the future direction of competitors.

If a competitor is a public company (on a stock exchange), you can review their financials and their annual reports. This can tell you who their new customers are and how they are performing. It will also help you understand their business model and strategies.

Competitive Sales Cycles

Sometimes a prospect will come right out and ask you who your competitors are.

This is a question that does not deserve a serious answer. We would typically name one competitor whose price was at least double ours and say they were our single biggest competitor.

Once a sales cycle begins, discreetly ask prospects if they're considering anyone else. If they say they are looking at someone else, ask them if they would mind sharing what other companies they are considering. At least 50 percent will tell you who they're considering and why.

Knowing your competition will help you plan your strategy and tactics to win the deal.

It is often good to (subtly) plant a "land mine" for a competitor. For example, when commenting on a competitor, you might say, "We know them well; a few of their employees have come to work for us in the last sixty days," or "We are familiar with them; we just converted XYZ Company off their platform and onto ours."

Assuming this is factually correct, this will create some FUD (fear, uncertainty, and doubt) in the mind of the prospect regarding your competitor. It will raise questions about viability and stability, and put the competitor on the defensive at some point during the sales cycle.

Do not bad-mouth your competition. This turns off many people and should be avoided at all costs. Even politicians are starting to realize that negativity regarding a competitor is not appreciated. It can backfire on you.

If you're selling against your competitors based on superior features and functions, make sure to stress the importance of what you do well that your competitors don't. Don't mention that competitors can't do X or Y, just talk about how your offering handles these scenarios and how it has benefited customers time and time again. That's always a good "land mine" for a competitor to deal with.

Our First Major Competitor: Greentree Software

When we started our software company, I knew from my experience as both a practitioner and a consultant that there was no other PC-based purchasing system like ours. I believed our P.O. Writer software from American Tech, Inc., was one-of-a-kind, and we were first to market.

I was wrong.

I had no idea another company had been developing a very similar product. About a year after we launched, one of our early customers called us and said he had just received a very nice brochure from Greentree Software in New York City. This was a surprise, and we didn't know what to make of this company. We asked our customer, a PhD in aeronautical engineering turned purchasing manager at Pitney Bowes, to send us the information packet he had received.

We were shocked and angered to see the packet. It included a cover letter with an endorsement from the National Association of Purchasing Managers (now ISM, or Institute of Supply Management). They touted Greentree's CAP (computer-aided purchasing) software as the only solution of its kind—something that would have a major impact on its members.

Not only did Greentree have an endorsement from the NAPM, but they had also recently done an IPO (initial public offering) and raised about $5 million. This was back in the day when almost anyone could go public, even "pre-revenue" companies. We were up against a company with access to capital and lots of it.

Our backs were against the wall. Frankly, we were concerned about our chances of successfully competing with a public company that had deep pockets and a major endorsement. There we were, a small company started with a little over $10,000 that had no endorsements of any kind, competing with a company with $5 million and an NAPM endorsement.

I was enraged that the NAPM could and would do such a thing. Part of what they preach is creating a "level playing field" for suppliers. I jumped on a plane at Detroit Metro Airport, flew to Newark, New Jersey, and drove a rental car to the NAPM headquarters, then in Oradell, New Jersey, for a meeting with its president.

He claimed that the mailing was not an endorsement but rather an educational initiative to introduce members to new technologies. I asked him if he would do the same for us and introduce P.O. Writer to the membership.

He said he would, but later changed his mind and never did give us a mention. He justified this by saying, "The NAPM no longer wants to educate our members on matters pertaining to technology." Apparently there were several other software companies that had reacted just as I did.

This ended the first of many run-ins with the NAPM over the years. We never figured out why they did what they did. We didn't have the time or money to figure it out. It was time to move on and crush our first major competitor.

Fortunately for us, the actual CAP product was buggy and not as robust as P.O. Writer. Greentree had beautiful marketing materials but did not display knowledge of the marketplace and the real world of purchasing.

Greentree and American Tech competed head-to-head for more than ten years. Early on, they had several opportunities to exploit some weaknesses in our product, but they never really took advantage of their position in the marketplace.

Greentree management was excellent at raising money from investors but not so good at developing, selling, and supporting their software. In fact, they managed to raise over $25 million during their seventeen-year history. Toward the end, they changed their name to PurchaseSoft, Inc., to change their image in the market.

They ceased operations after fifteen years with only two profitable years to show for all their advantages. We broke even after three years and were profitable twenty-two of the next twenty-five years.

Take-Away #32

Even if the deck is stacked against you, the SFE can prevail by staying focused on the marketplace.

How did we bring them down? They actually brought themselves down. As Woody Allen said, "90 percent of success is just showing up." We paid attention to our marketplace and our customers every day, while Greentree focused on Wall Street and raising more money.

The rigors of being a public company like Greentree are different from being an SFE like American Tech. Public-company CEOs spend about half their time dealing with raising capital, publishing quarterly and annual results, and dealing with investors. On the other hand, the SFE CEO can focus on the business of pleasing customers, building a great organization, and improving the product or service.

The other advantage the SFE has against the public company is access to the competitor's quarterly reports, annual reports, and press releases. Greentree tipped off many of their strategies and provided us with great fodder for planting "land mines" and creating FUD during competitive sales cycles.

We, on the other hand, could fly under the radar, and we took them by surprise numerous times.

Take-Away #33

David can beat Goliath. Focus on your customers and prospects every day, and an SFE can come out a winner over a public company.

Next Challenger: Verian Technologies

A new competitor entered the scene as Greentree was fading away. These folks received a significant venture-capital investment and developed a web-based product that was designed to compete with our new web-based product, PNet.

Although Verian got off to a slow start, we ended up competing with them on many deals. They were tough competitors because they were very flexible with their pricing, they were very good at planting "land mines" against us, their licensing model was simpler than ours, and they occasionally told a "mega sales truth" about their product. They covered their tracks quickly, however, by having their developers change the software to include that particular feature or function within a matter of days. They would then demonstrate the new software to the prospect to prove they could do it.

We each won 50 percent of the deals where we competed. They did help us build a better product and simplify our offering. We became easier to do business with as a result of Verian.

Take-Away #34

Figure out why you are losing sales to competitors and fix it. Competitors can make you a better company.

Selling to Existing Customers

One of the most important ways to ensure profitability is to maximize sales to current customers.

Studies have shown that it costs seven times as much to sell to a new customer as it does to sell to an existing customer. Sales cycles are much faster and profit margins are much higher when selling to your installed base.

As previously mentioned, when completing your initial sale to a customer, make every effort to pave the way for add-on sales. Selling an annual maintenance program is a great way to get started.

Building an ongoing relationship with your customer is also critical. We conducted an annual client forum and invited all of our customers to attend. There was a social aspect to the client forum (golf, sightseeing, etc.) as well as business meetings at which clients shared their ideas on how to improve our products and services. The forum helped build and maintain great relationships through the years.

Each year we gave ten "Client of the Year" awards in various categories. We presented trophies or plaques to the winners and runners-up in each category. They appreciated the gesture, and we generated lots of add-on business as a result. We used to say that the trophy was the best $50 investment we ever made. We also used photos of the winners to generate publicity on our website.

Take-Away #35

It costs seven times more to find and sell to a new customer than it does to sell more to an existing customer.

We also conducted customer-satisfaction surveys at the client forum and publicized the results during every sales cycle. We consistently received customer-satisfaction ratings of over 90 percent. Laurene and her team were instrumental in keeping our customers happy by providing great support and service. They consistently over-delivered.

We conducted an ongoing e-mail campaign to make sure our customers knew about new releases, new products, and new services. A monthly e-mail to each customer proved to be the best frequency for generating add-on business. Many of the e-mails included incentives, such as discounts and free services. Implementing a customer-loyalty program is an effective way to maximize sales to consumers.

Laurene also implemented an annual "client review" meeting with our biggest customers, at which we gave a presentation that covered milestones, accomplishments, and ROI (return on investment) statistics from the previous twelve months. We also shared our plans for the upcoming year so clients could align their resources. This allowed our contacts to educate their top management teams regarding our value proposition and future plans.

I was once told by a very successful SFE who had recently sold his company, "Make sure you get every possible dollar you can from your customers. Sell them as much as you can." This proved to be great advice.

Stay close to your customers, and you can maintain profitability.

Trade Shows

For us, exhibiting at trade shows was an expensive and ineffective way to market our products or services. We used to spend about $25,000 per show and rarely got a good return on our investment.

The only reason we ever went to a trade show was if all our primary competitors were going to be exhibiting, or if we were trying to penetrate a new vertical or horizontal market. For example, we exhibited at a Charter School Conference when we first tried to penetrate that vertical market. We exhibited at an Accounts Payable Conference when we first introduced our invoice-processing module. The results were questionable.

The only tangible benefit of a trade show is meeting potential business partners, resellers, OEMs, etc. I characterize a trade show as "sellers selling to sellers."

> ## Take-Away #36
>
> Try to avoid trade shows. If you must, attend an online virtual trade show and save your money.

Online Advertising

Before spending any money on online advertising with the likes of Google and Yahoo, concentrate your efforts on search-engine optimization techniques to get the highest possible ranking in the free listings. It may take nine to twelve months of continual tweaking of your website to rise to the first page of the search results for a given keyword or keyword phrase. Also, identify all the free sources of listings that can drive traffic to your website. Depending on the type of business you have this may include industry directories, LinkedIn, Twitter, and Facebook.

Once you have experienced diminishing returns on search engines' free listings (a.k.a. organic listings), consider being a "sponsor" of various keywords. The top three or four sponsors appear in sequence at the top of the page. Sponsors five and beyond are typically located on the right side of the search results.

The "paid rank" depends on how much you bid (in a continuous real-time auction). The highest bid is first, the next highest bid is second, and so on. You can save significant money by trying to rank second or third. Oftentimes, there is a significant difference in price between first and second, and the click-through rate is only slightly better for first.

You only pay the bid amount when someone actually clicks on your link and goes to your website.

There are several ways to control the amount of money you spend on this initiative. First, establish a daily budget. Your ad will no longer appear once your budget has been consumed.

Also, you can specify the days you want to be included or excluded from the sponsorship listings. You can also specify the time of day when you want to be included or excluded. For example, we excluded Saturdays and Sundays and from seven p.m. eastern to seven a.m. eastern. These were times that a good prospect probably wouldn't be looking for an automated purchasing system.

Another cost-saving measure is to periodically review each keyword or keyword phrase you are sponsoring to make sure that it is not only driving traffic to your website, but that the visitors are also being converted to leads or orders. We defined conversions as those visitors who requested additional information. They filled out a form on the website that included their contact information and a description of what they were looking for and what their current systems were. This represented a good, warm, high-quality lead.

All of this data (except the conversions) is available free on the search-engine website. It requires frequent review to maximize your online advertising dollar.

STAGE 3:

Achieving and Maintaining Profitability
Money

Cash Is King

Cash flow is the name of the game. On the revenue side of the equation, make sure you create incentives for on-time or early payment.

After we received an order, we delivered our software with full functionality but with a limit on the number of items that could be purchased. Once the customer paid the invoice, we supplied a password that removed the limitation and made the software useable in production for an unlimited number of items.

This proved to be a great way to improve cash flow. The customer wanted to pay on a timely basis.

Another example: When annual maintenance and support contracts were about to expire, we sent an invoice for the next year. We expected the invoice to be paid before the new term began. If payment was not received, the customer had to run with no support (help desk). We made no exceptions, and 95 percent of all customers did not want to take the risk of running in an unsupported mode. The result was timely payment and improved cash flow.

These techniques were unique to our business, but the principle of ensuring timely payments is critical to every business and every industry.

I used to say that the three things that kept me awake at night were not selling enough, not sending the invoices out on a timely basis, and not receiving the money on time.

This sounds like Business 101, but don't take any of it for granted. Make sure that invoice generation and payment receipt is the highest priority for a person (or department) in your company.

More companies are now using charge cards, prepaid cards, credit cards, and debit cards to pay invoices. You'll have to forgo 1 to 4 percent in order to get paid within twenty-four to forty-eight hours.

Traditionally, payment terms included a 2 percent discount for payment made in ten or fifteen days. The problem with this tactic is that the customer would take the 2 percent discount and pay late anyway.

On the expense side of the cash-flow equation, keep your overhead low and pay your suppliers just fast enough to maintain a good working relationship with them. Make sure your suppliers and contractors know your payment terms. For example, we told our suppliers the following: "We pay invoices on the fifteenth of every month. Your invoice will be paid on the pay date that falls thirty days after an accurate invoice is received."

For example, if you receive an accurate invoice on the fifth of May, you will pay it on the fifteenth of June. If you receive an accurate invoice on the seventeenth of May, it won't be paid until the fifteenth of July. If there is missing data or inaccurate data on an invoice, send it back to the supplier for correction. Once you receive a corrected invoice, the clock starts.

This policy will satisfy most suppliers if you communicate your process and set expectations. It will result in actual payment terms of thirty to sixty days.

For projects, negotiate milestone payments with a minimal down payment—one-third down followed by a one-third payment for completion of Phase I, followed by a one-third payment upon completion are typical payment terms for a project.

Take-Away #37

Simply stated, get the money in the door fast and part with it slowly. Maximize cash flow whenever possible.

One warning: *never, ever miss a payroll.* You can miss payment of almost anything except payroll. Your employees *must* get paid on time. Anything else is simply not acceptable. Late payroll isn't fair and will lead to severe morale problems within the company.

In twenty-eight years, I am proud to say we were never late on payroll. This paid big dividends in employee loyalty to our companies.

The Budgeting Fallacy

The problem with establishing and tracking expenses against an annual budget is that business conditions change too quickly for a budget to remain relevant. Don't spend too much time creating a budget. It is only a guide and shouldn't be used to influence spending behavior.

Bank Loans and Lines of Credit

Since you are now profitable, your bank looks at you in a different light. Assuming you are managing your personal finances responsibly, you should be able to get a business loan or line of credit, even if you don't need it. This is the banking way. They only lend money to people who can pay it back with 100 percent certainty.

In order to be a good bank customer and build up your credit worthiness, arrange for a small loan and repay it in its entirety almost immediately. It may cost you a few bucks in interest, but in the long run it is well worth the expense.

> ## Take-Away #38
>
> Banks love to loan money to people who don't need it and will pay it back immediately. It sounds illogical, but this is how you can become a valued bank customer. Someday you will need their help.

These are just short-term loans that can help smooth out the bumps in your cash flow. *Never* take a loan you know you can't easily pay back—and *never* consider taking a loan from someone who wants equity in your company.

At first, you will have to secure the loan or line of credit with savings or other assets, but in time, you will be able to borrow money with just your personal guarantee.

Save Your Money

For many of us, our profit from the business is the most money we have ever seen. In one way, it's exhilarating, and in another way, it's scary. At first, you aren't really sure what to do with it.

One thing *not* to do is spend it on fancy personal property, such as expensive clothing, cars, and boats. These things all depreciate in value and won't make you happier or a better person.

When you get ready to pay your bills, the first check you write should be to yourself. *Pay yourself first!* Pretend you are looking at a bill from yourself for $X per month. Where should this money go?

First, you will need to build your cash reserves (personally and in the company) so you can stop living hand-to-mouth and breathe a little easier. I tried to keep at least a six- to eight-week supply of cash in the company and build a six-month emergency fund at home.

Second, you'll need to reinvest in the company and build up enough capital to expand should you choose.

Third, state and federal tax bills need to be paid on a timely basis. Taxes are high and getting higher. Don't get surprised by unanticipated tax liabilities.

Fourth, you'll need to start saving money for your retirement. You may think it's too early, but it's never too early to start saving. Part of being an SFE is having the responsibility to self-fund your retirement. Social Security, even if it's still viable when you need it, isn't nearly enough to live on.

Even though you may feel rich as the cash piles up, when you get done saving for your retirement, it's not as much as you think.

How to Invest

I have been investing and managing "SFE money" for twenty-five years. I have learned a lot about investing during that time. Numerous books have been written on the subject. I recommend you read as many as time permits.

Some of the principles I have learned that I would recommend to any SFE:

1. *Diversify, Diversify, Diversify.* Try to spread your money around to cash, stocks, bonds, and other assets. Your own asset allocation percentages depend mostly on your age. The younger you are, the more you should have in stocks or ETFs (Exchange Traded Funds), and the less you should have in cash and bonds.

2. *Time Value of Money.* Understand the effect of compounding over many years. The $10,000 you invest today will be $20,000 in ten years (or so) if properly managed. Start investing as soon as you can. It will help pave the way to a comfortable retirement.

3. *Avoid "Exotic" Investments.* Don't invest in a friend's or relative's new business idea. You already have enough risk. I used to say that owning and running a business was like gambling every day.

4. *Spread Your Investments.* Don't put all your money in just one bank or brokerage. Spreading your money around helps minimize risk in the event of a severe recession or depression. It also will help you develop multiple sources of advice and guidance. Don't be afraid to use a discount brokerage—several have great online research and excellent customer service.

5. *Take Ownership of Your Investments.* If you lose money in the market, don't blame it on your broker. He or she doesn't care about your money as much as you do. You have the ultimate responsibility for your investments. Your broker or advisor can only make suggestions. Some suggestions you should reject and some you should accept. Regardless of what happens, you are responsible for the ultimate success or failure of your investments.

6. *Stay Educated.* You never know enough, and the world of finance is constantly changing. This means you need to learn something new every day by reading, watching TV, etc. Don't rely on your broker as your only source of information.

7. *Avoid "Hot Tips."* People love to talk about the latest hot stocks. Most of what you hear at cocktail parties and in locker rooms never works out, so ignore the chatter.

Take-Away #39

If it sounds too good to be true, it is too good to be true.

---

8. *Remember That Buying Is Easy and Selling Is Difficult.* If you decide to invest part of your free cash flow on a regular basis (monthly or quarterly) in an S&P index fund or ETF, you will be in good shape. When do you sell your fund or an individual stock? This is harder to figure out. When in doubt, sell half your position. If the stock goes up you'll feel good, and if it goes down you'll feel smart.

9. *Start a 401(k).* Do this for yourself and your employees. Fund your 401(k), profit-sharing, and other tax-deferred retirement accounts to the max first. Then put money into other bank and brokerage accounts.

10. *Buy Bonds.* Bonds and bond funds are good investments in times of steady or decreasing interest rates. Bonds are an "inverse operation." When interest rates go down, bonds go up in value. When interest rates go up, bond values decrease. Think of it this way: when interest rates go down, people are willing to pay more for the bonds you own (with higher interest rates) and less for newly issued bonds (with lower interest rates).

11. *Consider Annuities.* Annuities are worth considering if you're over forty-five years old. Some of the new variable annuities with guaranteed income riders are good additions to a retirement plan. They protect you from a down market and let you participate in a rising stock market. They have many "moving parts" and therefore are somewhat complex. Work with a licensed financial planner who specializes in annuities for help determining if annuities are appropriate for you.

You *will* make mistakes. We all make mistakes. The key is to learn from your mistakes, and never make the same mistake twice.

I made my share of mistakes. Like the time I "invested" (and lost) $15,000 in an oil-well-drilling exploration opportunity in Oklahoma. Or the time I "invested" (and lost) $10,000 in a complex options-trading strategy. Brilliant.

These episodes occurred early in my career, and I learned from them. I never made these mistakes again.

Taxes

Taxes are an anchor that weighs down every entrepreneur. Taxes are a cost of doing business—a rising cost. This cost acts as a drag on growth and profitability of every business.

What many politicians don't realize is that every SFE has a built-in auto-response to minimize the impact of cost increases. This response is to find a way to decrease costs to offset any cost increase. Every time taxes are increased, the SFE finds a cost reduction (or cost avoidance) to neutralize the impact of the cost increase.

It's like the old law of physics: "Every action has an equal and opposite reaction." The SFE can't help it—this is a built-in response to ensure profitability and positive cash flow no matter what is thrown at us.

Unfortunately, these added costs often result in layoffs or a reduction in employee hours. At the very least, it puts hiring plans on hold or results in a total cancellation of hiring plans.

I should emphasize that this "SFE reflex action" works automatically with *any* cost increase. That said, increasing taxes kills job growth. Small business needs to generate new jobs for our economy to grow. Increasing taxes is a guaranteed growth inhibitor.

To minimize the impact of taxes on the SFE, claim every possible (legitimate) expense to reduce taxable income. You can be very aggressive in your deductions. There's no reason to be conservative. The worst thing that will happen if you get audited (which is less than a 2 percent chance) is that your expenses will be reduced and you will have to pay a little more.

On the revenue side, *never, ever* under-report your revenue. If you intentionally under-report your company's revenue, you are leaving yourself open to major fines or even jail time.

Take-Away #40

Be very aggressive with legitimate expense deductions but *never* under-report your revenue. You might end up in jail.

Also, your accountant probably has many clients and can't think of every tax deduction and strategy that can save you money. Continue to read and learn about tax-saving ideas and run them by your accountant to see if they may help you. Every so often, you'll discover a little nugget that can help reduce your tax bill.

Double Your Prices and Keep Half Your Customers

My mentor, Hal Mather, once made this statement: "Every consultant should double their fees and hope to keep half of their customers." It was said somewhat tongue-in-cheek, but also makes a great point.

One way to increase margins is to increase prices. It is also a way to get rid of marginal and unprofitable customers. Instead of hiring additional consultants, raising prices will allow you to increase revenue with the same manpower level.

At the very least, "fire" your worst customers every year. This will rid you of the real "time sucks" and allow you to focus your efforts on strategically important customers.

Pay Employees Frequent Bonuses

Rather than pay selected managers a significant annual bonus, pay smaller and more frequent bonuses to everyone. This approach will cost less and generate more good will than you can imagine. These bonuses can be paid for great performance or extraordinary efforts.

This can even help eliminate complex, expensive incentive-compensation plans that may benefit a few managers and salespeople, but infuriate everyone else.

Salespeople say they need incentive compensation (commissions) to stay motivated. In thirty years, I saw no evidence that money, in itself, motivates anyone. But the act of personally recognizing people for their contributions with a (small) bonus does motivate almost everyone receiving a bonus.

We tried to return 15 percent of our net income (after taxes) to our employees in the form of bonuses and contribution to the company profit-sharing plan. It helped us retain our best employees and allowed us to remain profitable for many years.

Stage 3:

Achieving and Maintaining Profitability
Management

Mind-Set	Marketing	Money	Management

Building the Organization

As you reach the break-even point, you are now in a position to build your organization. The motivation to build the organization may be to support future growth, maintain profitability and positive cash flow, or add some depth to the organization so you can rebalance your personal priorities.

Regardless of the reason, now is a good time to build your management team. As the company grows, decisions need to be made differently. In the previous phase, the SFE made all the decisions. Now decisions will be made through collaboration and consensus. You can still be a benevolent dictator if you so chose, but you'll need to get others involved. Even the greatest athletes need a good team around them in order to win. You'll need a good team too.

Let Go!

One of the big reasons entrepreneurs can't maintain profitability is the inability to let go. They just can't (or won't) delegate responsibilities to others in the organization. This behavior must be changed before building your team. What's the purpose of hiring a LeBron James if you won't pass the ball to him?

Why won't some SFEs let go? The reasons include an attitude that "No one can do this as well as I can," or perhaps it's a feeling that "My neck is on the line, so I'll do it."

My partner, being one of the most polite people I know, sometimes hesitated to delegate to others because they were "too busy" and she didn't want to overload them.

Laurene had difficulty delegating because she felt that if she wasn't exactly sure how to do something herself, she couldn't explain it to someone else. But delegating doesn't necessarily mean telling someone how to do something.

Delegating involves describing the objective, the desired end result (the deliverable), the desired completion date with key milestones, and the relative priority versus other tasks. Many great managers don't know how to get things done and don't really care how they get done! A good manager doesn't need to micromanage anybody—just get results.

Assembling Your Team

When we were starting up our software company, I asked a successful SFE who had experience hiring programmers and analysts how much he had to pay to hire one. He told me that he could hire a contract programmer for between $25 and $200 per hour—quite a large range.

He then surprised me by stating that given a choice, he would hire the $200 per hour programmer *every time*. He went on to explain that the $200-per-hour person got the job done quickly with excellent quality. The $25-per-hour person typically made many mistakes, required more time to manage, and took more time to complete the project. Now, based on thirty years of my own experience, I would agree with everything he said. Our higher-paid programmers consistently created proportionally more value than our lower-paid programmers.

Many American businesses are now being "forced" by competition to hire low-cost employees. I would resist this temptation when hiring your management team. In most cases, it's better to spend a little more to get the best available candidate. In the long run, you will probably receive more value from the more expensive person. Admittedly, this is a hard thing to do with limited funds, but with positive cash flow, you'll get over it quickly.

That said, the single most important thing to look for in a management candidate is that you believe you will be comfortable working together. That doesn't necessarily mean you agree on every topic, but simply that you can work together and you share the same values. Make sure the new manager will be a good fit for *your* company.

We found that the profile of a good manager at our company was someone who had worked for a large organization *and* a small organization, *and* had applicable industry experience. The reasons these attributes were important:

- **Experience in a Large Company:** The new manager has learned business processes and management practices that will help you maintain profitability. Although much has been learned at big companies, this manager prefers working for a smaller organization. Also, since our customers were large companies, this experience helped the manager relate to our customers.

- **Experience in a Small Company:** The manager knows what it's like to operate in a hands-on mode with a small (or no) support staff. He or she can work independently and likes the feeling of contributing to the success of the company—a feeling you tend to get more often at a small company.

- **Applicable Industry Experience:** It is very unusual for someone to leave one industry and make a fast, successful transition to another industry. For example, it is difficult to make the change from a manufacturing industry to a service industry or vice versa.

Of course, there is a long list of potential red flags. The most common red flags are a sloppy resume with grammar and/or spelling mistakes, any statement (written or verbal) that turns out not to be truthful, or a criminal record of any kind.

It is difficult to look past any of these red flags.

Beyond this, the most important thing is that there is good chemistry between you and a potential team member. Trust your gut on this one.

I always wanted any potential team member to be interviewed by a number of other people in the company. This gives the candidate a better idea of what it would be like to work for you. It also generates feedback from other people. If the chemistry is good among them, you've got a viable candidate. Invariably, your current people will help recruit the candidate if they like him or her.

As my partner Laurene put it, "The people who do well at our company are the ones who can work independently and don't need to be managed. People who need micromanaging or constant praise never fit in very well here."

We wanted to hire very smart people who would work well in a collegial environment like ours.

What If You Make a Hiring Mistake?

If you think hiring a bad employee is a problem, you can't imagine the impact of hiring a bad middle manager with his or her own agenda. One individual's weaknesses are amplified and spread throughout the organization.

Upon hiring a new member of your management team, develop a learning-curve plan with key milestones and share it with the new manager. Some new managers are a perfect fit, have applicable experience, and can hit the ground running. Others require more time to learn more about your industry, your company, and your processes.

This plan will help you both understand expectations and timelines. I've hired a sales manager who was productive on Day 1. I've also hired an executive who I knew would take six to nine months to come up to speed. Team members need to be handled individually based on their backgrounds and expertise.

Once you have shared the plan, tracked progress, and communicated deficiencies, if improvement is not forthcoming, it's time to move in another direction.

For departing managers, try to give them a heads-up that you will be making a change. As long as they can keep doing their job and aren't disruptive, allow them some time (two to three months) to find another position. It's much easier to find a job when you have a job.

You owe him or her that much.

One condition of continued employment is if they tell anyone else (in the company) about their situation, they will be terminated on the spot. I've given a heads-up probably twenty times and only had one or two problems.

Take-Away #41

Make sure new managers understand your expectations for how fast they should come up the learning curve.

Once you know you've made a mistake, take action and move on. The cost of not taking action is loss of profits and cash flow. The SFE simply can't tolerate a bad hire.

Managing Managers

Let your managers manage their own people and projects. That's why you hired them. Let them do their job. On the other hand, you can't delegate and "forget about it."

That raises the question: "How do you know they are doing their jobs well without looking over their shoulders all the time?"

- First, establish an annual performance plan that you both buy into.

- Second, create daily, weekly, or monthly measurements to ensure objectives are being met.

- Third, communicate as often as the manager needs. Some need lots of interaction and others don't. Not everyone can be managed the same way.

- Fourth, have a regularly scheduled thirty- to sixty-minute meeting with your team once a week to discuss progress and coordinate activities.

- Fifth, use a technique called MBWA: Management by Walking Around. I tried to walk through the entire company almost every day around 3:00 p.m. It's amazing what you will see and hear. You'll learn a lot about your own company and how your people are performing. Of course, if everyone is in a remote location, it is a little difficult to implement this technique.

Top Ten SFE Management Principles for Maintaining Profitability

1. *Leverage everything you do.* Every time you provide a service, make every effort to "productize" that service and offer it to other prospects and customers. Include the new service on your price list, if you publish one.

2. *Progressive improvement beats the hell out of postponed perfection.* The important thing is to take action to do something now! It doesn't have to be perfect, and you'll never have all the information you need.

3. *"Go ugly early" and reevaluate and adjust frequently.* Do something every day to move the business forward, and reevaluate your approach and processes frequently. Ask yourself, "In light of everything I know today, does what we're doing still make sense?"

4. *Trust your gut.* You're going to be working with imperfect, incomplete information every day, so you'll need to trust your gut many times every day. If you're lucky (and good), you'll be right more than you're wrong.

5. *Consult.* Seek input from your management team, board of advisors, customers, etc., to make sure you're moving in the right direction. You'll never make everyone happy, especially customers. I used to say "Customers are always right 50 percent of the time."

6. *Profitability is critical.* There are many objectives to consider when running a business. Many of them are conflicting objectives. If you're in doubt about a decision, use profitability potential as the tiebreaker.

7. *Employees are your biggest asset.* On a balance sheet, "plant and equipment" may appear as one of your biggest assets, but your people are what differentiate you from your competitors.

8. *Treat employees with respect.* Keep in mind each has different wants and needs. Some will be hard-charging, and some will be more concerned about their kid's next soccer game. When in doubt, over-communicate with each of them to figure out how to create a win-win environment.

9. *Hire the best employees you can possibly afford.* This is one area where it can make sense to overspend. If you can get a superior candidate for an additional 15 percent or 20 percent and the individual is a good fit, go for it. It will pay off sooner than you think.

10. *Make sure you have a strong "money person" on your team.* Cash flow is the name of the game. This person can have the title of chief financial officer, controller, or bookkeeper—the title doesn't matter as long as he or she can help create and maintain positive cash flow.

STAGE 4:

The Growth Stage
Mind-Set

Mind-Set	Marketing	Money	Management

> *This is my quest, to follow that star ...*
> *No matter how hopeless, no matter how far ...*
>
> *To try ... when your arms are too weary ...*
> *To reach ... the unreachable star ...*
>
> **The Impossible Dream**
> Written by Joe Darion

Reasons for Growing

Now that you've reached profitability, you are in a position to make some very important decisions regarding the growth trajectory of your company. Being an SFE (self-funded entrepreneur) gives you many options.

Some SFEs choose to continue operating at roughly the same level of business, run the business for cash, and live happily ever after—what's often called a "lifestyle business." Other SFEs choose to step on the gas and expand the business.

Still others choose to get the company ready for sale and move on.

We decided to grow the company's revenues to increase the value of the business. We also wanted to build the company in such a way that it continued to be profitable. We followed a very simple rule: this year's expenses must be lower than last year's revenues. This would ensure profitability as long as revenues increased over the previous year. We described this as our "profitable growth strategy."

Using this approach, we grew at a CAGR (compound annual growth rate) of 21 percent and achieved profitability in twenty-two of twenty-four years. During that time, we grew annual revenues from $300,000 to $7 million.

Take-Away #42

Our rule: this year's total expenses must be less than last year's revenues.

The reasons we decided to grow the company were:

1. To increase cash flow. With gross margins of 80 percent, each incremental sales dollar generated 80 cents of positive cash flow.

2. In a technology business, you either move ahead or fall back. We didn't want to fall back.

3. There was a large growing market, and we wanted a piece of it.

4. The value of any business is determined (in part) by its growth rate. Software businesses are valued at a multiple of sales. Common multiples for company valuations are 2X–3X sales. Growing the company would increase the value of the business.

5. It was a great challenge, and SFEs love challenges.

We were tempted to take on outside investors to maximize our growth. (More about that in "Money.")

If you consider leaving the ranks of the SFEs, now is the time to take on an equity partner.

The reason: if rapid growth is important to you, self-funding may not be the best way to accomplish this objective. There are limits to how fast you can grow using the self-funded model.

For example, if your primary objective is to go public through an IPO (Initial Public Offering), now is the time to seek investors.

At one point, we thought we wanted to go in this direction. Pre-revenue companies were going public. We started to develop "IPO envy" and thought, "Why shouldn't we go for it?"

Understanding Venture Capitalists

I spent the better part of two years looking for the right venture capitalist (VC). I never found one, but I learned a lot in the process.

I actually looked at about twenty of them. It was smack in the middle of the Internet boom. I remember being chauffeured around Wall Street accompanied by two investment bankers and dashing in and out tall buildings to meet with potential investors. Visions of an IPO and instant wealth made this an exhilarating time.

Truth be told, when it comes to getting venture capital, timing is everything—and we were a little late to the party. The VC community likes to invest in a total of three or four companies in a given category (or "space" as they call it), and over four companies had already received VC backing in the B2B eCommerce and eProcurement space. It turned out to be a blessing in disguise that we never took VC money.

Circa 1997, VCs were looking for companies with a "hockey stick" forecast that reflected hyper-growth. At that time, profitability meant nothing. The name of the game was top-line growth. I remember one young VC who had just reviewed our numbers and had a very puzzled look on his face. He turned to me and asked, "Why are you running your company to make a profit?"

I was stunned and speechless.

Wasn't profitability a primary objective of owning and operating a business?

This young fellow went to a very prestigious university, so he must have learned something that I never knew. Maybe he was taught that losing money was a good thing.

Giving him the benefit of the doubt, I think he was suggesting that if we had run the business at a loss, we would have reinvested more money in the business, and this would have resulted in accelerated growth.

When you get appointments with VCs, you'll typically see bright young MBAs who have never made a payroll in their life. They are very good at "slicing and dicing" data and calculating ratios. These "junior jocks" are nice, polite, well-educated people, but they should have gotten a real job first.

Take-Away #43

Only consider VC and other outside investment once you are profitable and have decided to grow rapidly and shoot for an IPO.

At the time we were meeting with VCs, capital was so plentiful that they didn't want to invest the $5 million we were looking for—they wanted to invest more!

One VC said to me, "I know you are looking for $5 million, but what could you do if we gave you $10 or $15 million instead? What could you do with that capital?"

Once again, I was stunned. I said, "I don't think I could spend that amount effectively in a one-year period. It would be like throwing money out the window." Meeting over.

You have to understand where VCs are coming from. They want you to spend the money quickly and show results within a year or less. One time a bright Ivy Leaguer lectured me. He said, "If one sales rep has a sales quota of $1.3 million, and you hire ten new sales reps, you will generate $13 million per year in revenue."

Thanks for the math lesson.

This sounds good, but it's not so easy. He should have been asking where the leads would come from and what's needed to convert them to actual sales. Also, I could count on one hand the number of salespeople I have known who consistently met or exceeded quota.

The Odds

The VCs are hoping to have one or two very successful investments out of every ten they make. The other eight or nine are in danger of getting flushed if they don't progress quickly toward an IPO or acquisition.

VCs will want about 30–40 percent of your company in return for their initial investment. When the company is eventually sold, they'll want their money first. You'll get paid last, and there may not be anything left after they've taken their share.

VCs will tell you they can do "so much more than just give you money." They'll say they have lots of operational experience in your industry and can bring you lots of new customers.

Most can't. VCs will want seats on your board of directors and will have you tied up in knots in no time. You will become a prisoner in your own company.

Many VCs will tell you they'll invest if you can find another VC to "lead the investment." This is so they can minimize their risk without doing any work.

Take-Away #44

"In the US, a person has a better chance of winning a million dollars or more in a state lottery than getting VC to launch a new business."
Source: The Global Entrepreneurship Monitor's 2009 Report

In summary, in the vast majority of cases, it's not worth it. You can, and will, be very successful without them. Don't consider bringing on outside investors unless you want to grow more than 25 percent per year. Up to 25 percent can be done the old fashioned way—through positive cash flow, satisfying real customers, and hard work.

Stage 4:

The Growth Stage

Marketing

Going Global

If you make the decision that you want to grow, the next big question is *how* do you want to grow? Do you want to grow organically or through acquisition? Do you want to grow globally or domestically?

In the software business, about 50 percent of total worldwide revenues are generated within the US, and 50 percent come from outside the United States. That makes it very tempting to grow a US-based business by going global.

We decided to expand by addressing English-speaking markets outside the United States. This included Canada, the UK, Australia, and Singapore. We wanted to find one reseller in each country that could help us penetrate these markets.

We found a small consulting firm in the UK and one in Australia. They seemed to be competent and well-established in their area of expertise, which was supply-chain management—a closely related field.

In Singapore, we found a company run by an American who would create a major presence for us in Asia, first in Singapore and then in Japan. It was to be run as a joint venture, with both companies putting up $250,000. Ultimately, we would buy "PurchasingNet Asia" from them once the new entity became profitable.

Although the owner seemed reputable, it turned out that they were underfunded and went out of business in nine months.

We had spent countless hours educating, training, and supporting them, and they ended up generating no revenue. We did learn a few things about going global, however. Let me share them with you.

First, differences in culture have a dramatic effect on how you operate outside the United States. For example, one question we would ask US prospects was, "What problems are you hoping to solve by implementing our software?" When we asked this question at a sales call in Singapore, it was met with dead silence. After rephrasing the question, we were told that they had no problems. The meeting went downhill from there.

We were later told by our local partner that admitting to having problems was considered a sign of weakness in that society, and no one wanted to look weak.

Another example occurred after presenting our software to a group of over 100 prospects in Singapore at a breakfast seminar at a local hotel. I concluded by asking if there were any questions. The group was very engaged during my presentation, but no one would ask a question. Eventually, we got a couple of questions, but were told later that people there are hesitant to ask questions in a group (another sign of weakness?). People would only ask questions in private.

Second, if you're going to invest any money in a joint venture, you need to check the financials of the other company. I did not dig deep enough, and it turned out to be a huge mistake. They were funded by some well-heeled investors in Europe with "deep pockets," but once the economy started to slow and the Internet bubble started to burst, these investors wouldn't put any more money into the company. That's why they had deep pockets. They wouldn't throw good money after bad.

We found out through one of the ten employees hired for our joint venture that they hadn't gotten paid in almost two months. The employees had signed a contract to not communicate any bad news directly to us, and the only reason one took the risk and called us is because she was afraid of losing her home—the government of Singapore holds the mortgages and collects the payment from the employer. The company had run out of money and had ceased operations. We lost all of our investment.

If I had to do it all over again, I would have done more financial due diligence. I would have looked into their funding situation to ensure they could stay alive for at least two years. By then, the joint venture would have either been up and running or dissolved.

Take-Away #45

If you decide to go global, make sure you control your own destiny. Open your own office and hire your own people.

The best way to control your own destiny is by opening your own offices in countries you are targeting for expansion. Hire people familiar with the culture and the nuances of doing business in that country.

And you need at least one manager you know and trust.

Instead of hiring ten employees, we would have opened a small office staffed by two or three people (one sales rep, one marketing person, and one technical person). It probably would have cost us the same amount and would have given us a much better chance of being successful.

It wasn't a total loss. I appeared on CNBC (Asia) and on a Singapore TV business channel for an interview. We later used footage as a promotional tool in the States. It was a great personal experience for me.

We frequently reflect back on our ten-day visit to Singapore (with a weekend in Hong Kong). We have great memories. As I like to say, "It was the most exciting $250,000 trip ever!"

Selling to Current Customers

A far more profitable way to grow is to concentrate on expanding the usage of your product or service by your current customers.

As mentioned previously, it costs five to seven times as much to sign a new customer as it does to sell add-on business to a current customer.

Make sure to e-mail something of value to each of your customers every month. Include an incentive for them to buy more products or services from you. This is a very low-cost way to stay in touch with your customers and educate them through articles, case studies, surveys, and statistics. This can be done for less than $20 a month.

In certain industries, an annual customer meeting where all customers come together with you and your staff is an extremely effective way to build relationships and grow add-on business. This get-together can be online or in person.

We had a client forum every year in a different city (Las Vegas was always the most popular). We had some fun with our customers and learned firsthand what they were looking for in the way of new software modules and services. It also gave us the opportunity to share our vision of the future and educate/train them on soon-to-be-released software and services.

The other thing we did to maximize sales to our current customers was to stratify or rank our customer base. "A" customers were strategically important and offered the best opportunity to increase revenue. "B" customers were good midsize customers with modest upside potential. "C" customers were small or not likely to expand.

We sent a team to visit our "A" customers twice a year. The customer received a customized account review presentation once a year. "B" customers were visited once a year by our account manager. "C" customers were visited via conference call once a year by our professional-services group.

The combination of monthly e-mails, client forums, and customer stratification program provided over 30 percent compounded annual growth within our customer base over a twenty-year period. At one point, 65 percent of our revenue came from our existing installed base. This was one of the ways we grew while surviving five recessions.

Buzz

Now is the time to create some buzz.

Turn up the heat on your SEO (search-engine optimization) efforts and start looking at sponsoring various keywords in Google, Yahoo, and other search engines. Hopefully by now you've gained enough experience with search engines to know what's working and not working in your industry. Since you have achieved profitability, you now have some money to spend on SEM (search-engine marketing) or paid search.

Make sure you are ready for all the new leads you will be generating. Leads are worthless if you can't respond to them quickly and professionally. In most cases, this will require a phone call in addition to an autorespond e-mail.

Customer case studies are the best way to get attention from the media. The reason they are so powerful is that customers, prospects, media, and analysts are suspicious of everything a company says about itself. However, when a customer speaks, everyone listens. Case studies can be the basis for a great PR campaign or article in a relevant publication. A good format for a case study is:
- Description of the customer
- Problem the customer was experiencing prior to buying your product or service
- Impact of these problems on the customer's life or business
- How your product or service solved the problem
- Implementation experience with your firm (on time, on budget)
- Benefits experienced by the customer
- Quote from the customer (when possible, use actual names of the company and the customer)

It is now very easy to produce a video case study and publish it on your website. This can be done in interview format and is a very cost-effective tool.

If your product or service is sold to consumers rather than businesses, use

Facebook, Twitter, and other social networks to get your case studies in front of customers and prospects.

Business Development

During your growth stage, you will attract and recruit companies that can resell your product or service and refer business to you. In order to determine if they are the right partners for you, you will have to perform due diligence. Here was our due diligence checklist (questionnaire):

1. Product/Service Offerings
2. Business Model
3. Technology
4. Revenue Breakdown (by Product/Service)
5. Employees by Department
6. Customers (Names)
7. Last Win
8. Competitive Advantages
9. Best Win
10. Markets Serviced
11. Funding Sources
12. Profitability (Income Statements and Balance Sheets)
13. Competitors
14. Synergies
15. Common Customers between You and Them
16. Product Pipeline
17. Average Deal Size
18. Market Size
19. Management Bios
20. Value Proposition

Make sure you do your homework before selecting partners. They will require lots of time and attention, so make sure they'll be a good fit before making a commitment.

Qualifying Prospects

One of the most important and trickiest tasks in sales management is qualifying prospective customers.

It is important to qualify each prospect so you don't waste valuable time with prospects that will never buy your product or service. Conversely, you'll want to focus all of your attention on the good prospects who can, and will, buy your product or service.

You can usually qualify a prospect by asking a few questions to determine if they have the need, money, authority, and knowledge to buy your product or service.

We tried our best to avoid "chasing rabbits." We were ruthless in qualifying prospects.

The good news is we didn't waste much time. The bad news is we occasionally goofed and didn't pursue sales opportunities that eventually bought software from a competitor. The US Postal Service was one example. Because of their size and reputation for moving slowly, we decided not to respond to their request for proposal. They ended up signing a $5 million contract with a competitor half our size. Ouch!

I wish we had pursued this business. We probably could have won the deal. We all learn from our mistakes. Our mistake here was not building a relationship with the prospect and disqualifying them based on our quantitative analysis only.

STAGE 4:

The Growth Stage

Money

September 11

September 11, 2001, was one of the worst days in American history. I think this day represented the biggest single failure of my (Baby Boomer) generation. How could we have let this happen?

That day, I felt like all the great things the Boomers had accomplished were suddenly irrelevant. I took it very personally. We visited Ground Zero two weeks after the attacks, and I sobbed like a baby when looking at the pictures of the missing or deceased posted on a wall near the site of the attack.

My next-door neighbor was at work at Cantor Fitzgerald in the Twin Towers when the planes hit. He did not survive the terrorist attacks.

Almost 3,000 people died that day. That day, the world changed forever. Business slowed to a crawl for months and years following the September 11 attacks.

The impact on our business was (almost) devastating. We had gone down the path of getting outside funding and had worked with an investment-banking firm that had arranged $1.2 million in temporary financing (convertible notes) so we could accelerate our growth while looking for permanent financing. In addition, we had arranged for a line of credit with Merrill Lynch and had drawn down about $300K to fund our growth plans.

The $1.2 million temporary financing was orchestrated by Janney Montgomery Scott in Philadelphia. The money was raised from fourteen

123

individual investors who invested anywhere from $25,000 to $250,000 each.

We agreed to repay the notes (with 9 percent interest) after one year or the investors could (individually) convert their notes to equity in our company, PurchasingNet, Inc.

The notes were signed in September of 2000. The notes were due on September 19, 2001. The first week of September, 2001, I was told by Janney's investment banking department that they had been in touch with each of the fourteen investors and all of them planned to convert their notes to equity.

I was about to leave the ranks of the self-funded entrepreneurs. I was on the verge of meeting my fourteen new partners.

Or so I thought.

The day after September 11, my representative at Janney reiterated that everyone was going to convert to equity and own stock in the company.

On September 14, I started getting calls from the investors asking for their money back ASAP. By September 19, thirteen of the investors indicated they wanted their money *immediately*. One "gave me" ninety-day terms to pay the note.

It turns out that eight of the fourteen investors had roots in the Middle East. One of the Janney brokers who was also originally from the Middle East had raised money from these eight individuals. After September 11, each of these investors wanted their money back immediately. I had taken a couple of calls myself from these investors. One actually said that "the world is coming to an end." They were frantic to say the least.

So was I. For the next year, I felt like I had my head stuck in a vise. I had $1.3 million in debt, and the software industry had entered a "nuclear winter" following September 11.

I didn't have anything near $1.3 million in cash on hand. As a further kick in the teeth, when I got home the evening of October 1, a FedEx letter from Merrill Lynch was sitting on my front steps. The letter demanded immediate payment (by 5:00 p.m. the next day!) of the total line of credit. That added $300K to the debt to bring the total to $1.6 million.

Turns out the Merrill Lynch letter actually had nothing to do with September 11. They wanted me to pay off (clean up) the line at least once a year based on the terms of the agreement. I made three or four calls and eventually found someone at Merrill Lynch who could make a decision to extend the line. I got a one-year extension and an apology for not talking to me before their demand arrived at the front door.

Luckily, Michael Mufson, the head of the investment banking department at Janney, had just moved over to Commerce Bank and quickly arranged for a $1.5 million line of credit at Commerce Bank (now TD Bank). Here's the benefit of having saved money and kept our expenses in line—we had the means to back up this line of credit and Mike knew it. The lesson learned: don't overextend yourself when you start making money!

By the way, I don't blame Michael or Janney for what happened. If the September 11 attacks hadn't taken place, I never would have had to pay the notes off. In the long run, however, this was a blessing in disguise.

Rebuilding

Looking back at it, I could have tried to negotiate the individual payoffs and paid a fraction of the face value of the notes. This experience was new to me, and for the first time in my career, I was like a deer in the headlights. I didn't know what to do, so I did what the agreement called for: repay the notes with 9 percent interest. We paid off all of the notes (with interest) and worked down the line of credit over the next three years.

We explored several permanent financing alternatives. We met with the EVP of Commerce Bank, and he summarized our situation very accurately at the end of our meeting:

> "You don't like debt. You don't like being here. You don't need to be here. You raised some money. You took a shot. You went for the ring. Shit happens. Now you want to reverse this and go back to making a few hundred thousand a year and running your company the way it was before."

In the midst of all this chaos, our auditing firm PriceWaterhouseCoopers (PWC) started talking about giving us a "going concern" statement that essentially would say that there was a risk our company might go out of business.

This would have stopped companies from buying our products. It would have been a self-fulfilling prophecy. It would have been nails in the coffin.

This was the worst three weeks of my life.

It felt as though everyone was turning on me. I had no control. The vise on my head was closing a little more every day. It was like a bad dream. I was afraid we would lose it all.

This was supposed to be our growth stage, and now we were suddenly laying off people and cutting costs just to survive.

"You went for the ring. Shit happens." That phrase never left me. I might add my own saying: "There's no such thing as a free lunch." Once you take money from anyone, you're on the hook. That is why being an SFE is so cool. You control your own destiny.

THE VISE

Board

Bankers   Partners

Customers   Employees

Prospects   Suppliers

2001–2003

This was the scariest period of my thirty-year entrepreneurial life. We were supposed to be growing, but we were shrinking.

The "SFE reflex action" kicked in. I had to figure out a way to offset this pain. I decided to use this slow time to build a new product line we called PNet ePayables. I knew there wouldn't be an immediate payback, but while the "nuclear winter" existed in the software industry, we could use our time and resources to create a product that would revolutionize the way invoices are processed and paid.

This averted several layoffs and positioned us for growth once the overall business climate improved—which it did in 2004.

VC Postmortem

In retrospect, what we could have done differently was spin off a new company and keep our current company focused on existing PC-based software customers. The new company could have hired a high-powered management team (Harvard and Stanford MBAs) and started up as a pre-revenue company concentrating on web-based eProcurement. We could have retained partial interest in the new company and sat on the board of directors.

If we had done this in 1997 or 1998, it might have resulted in an IPO for the new company. Worst case, the new company wouldn't have survived long-term, but we would have profited from an IPO and still owned our original company.

One thing I have learned about the world of finance is that you are only limited by your own imagination. If you can think of it, you can find someone to finance it (when you're in a position of power).

The other thing I learned was that all you can do is make the best possible decisions based on the best information available at that point in time.

No Monday-morning quarterbacking. Just make something happen and move forward. That's what we always tried to do.

STAGE 4:

The Growth Stage

Management

Mind-Set	Marketing	Money	Management

Goal-Setting

Whether you are still an SFE or have taken on outside investors, you'll need to set goals and develop forecasts as you continue to grow.

There are different philosophies about goal-setting. Some believe that establishing "stretch goals" or "setting the bar high" is the way to go. The thinking is that if the goal or forecast is too low, people won't push themselves or work as hard.

Avoiding the Hockey Stick

It is "stretch goals" thinking that supports the "hockey stick" forecasting mentality.

For the SFE, this is absurd. Setting unrealistically high goals just leads to frustration, distorted priorities, and overspending to support this crazy forecast.

I don't care how much funding you have, it is very doubtful you can hit this forecast. You're only kidding yourself.

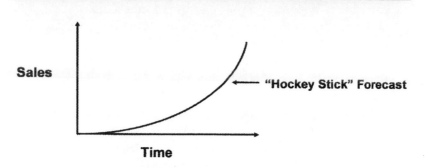

It is far better to establish a realistic, achievable, yet moderately aggressive forecast. Your team should participate in the development of goals and forecasts. You want them to sign up for these goals. They can then be used as a meaningful measurement of performance.

The more important task is to determine how you're going to achieve the goal or forecast. What resources are needed? What strategies and tactics are needed? Who will be responsible and take ownership of the tasks at hand?

It's the "how to" and the commitment to the goals that is important.

The actual numerical forecast is very important for a publicly owned company. Wall Street lives and dies on meeting the forecast and Wall Street's expectations.

To the SFE, the accuracy of the forecast itself is not life or death. A forecasting guru named Oliver Wight once said, "Forecasts fall into two categories, lousy and lucky, and there aren't too many that are lucky."

Ten Ways to Deal with Entrepreneurial Stress

It can be lonely and stressful at the top of the organization chart. Here are ten ways to manage the stress that every SFE experiences from time to time.

1. *Realize that the only person who can put pressure on you is* you. Have you ever noticed that some people let criticism just roll off their backs while others are greatly affected by criticism? The difference is in how you handle criticism, pressure, and adversity.
2. *Don't worry about what you can't control.* Focus on what you can control.

3. *Compartmentalize stress when necessary.* If there's a problem at work, leave it at work and don't bring it home with you. This is particularly important if your partner is your spouse.

4. *When dealing with a severely stressful or intense situation, take one day at a time.* Work your way through it. Don't try to predict what tomorrow will bring. Just put your head down and work through the day.

5. *Plan your day based on what works for you.* Working fifteen hours a day won't necessarily help you through stressful times. In fact, it may make things worse. I used to work in the office from 7:30 a.m. to 3:00 p.m. and then go work out or play golf. After dinner, I would typically work two to three hours and concentrate on longer-range issues. This schedule worked for me and kept me sane, especially during times of stress.

6. *Delegate as much as you can.* You need a way to offload as much work as possible so you can concentrate on the critical strategies that will minimize stress and help you meet your goals for growth and continued profitability.

7. *Maintain a written to-do list and continually reprioritize tasks.* Designate each task as an A, B, or C item, with the A items being the most critical and the C being the least important.

8. *Accept that it's okay not to be perfect.* Not everything you say or do needs to be perfect. Lower your standards a bit, especially during stressful times.

9. *Spend at least an hour a day exercising.* Lifting weights in particular is a great way to help manage stress.

10. *Consider how lucky you are to be where you are, doing what you're doing.* Compared to people slaving away in the corporate world, life is good.

Stock Options

During the Internet boom of the late 1990s, many companies created stock-option plans to attract talented people and provide incentives to grow the company. Even privately owned companies like ours created stock-option plans to compete for the best talent.

When we established our original stock-option plan, we set an expiration date of ten years in the future. This seemed like an adequate period of time, as we expected to IPO or sell the company by then. It is amazing how quickly ten years can fly by when you are running a company and raising a family.

When the plan expired, we had a few choices: continue to offer a regulated stock-option plan, subject to the new IRA regulations in effect at that time, or create a new plan that we could roll existing stock-option holders into with similar tax consequences. We chose the latter, switching to a homegrown LIP (loyalty incentive program) that was similar to our expiring stock-option plan. It provided key people with an incentive to stay with the company. As with a stock-option plan, employees were given a certain number of LIPs at the discretion of management. They vested over five years. Employees forfeited them if they left the company.

When the company was sold, the employees with LIPs participated in the sale by receiving a percentage of the value of the company. It was a nice way to say thank you and reward them for their loyalty.

Ethics

If you have to tell someone that you're ethical, you probably aren't. Ethics can't be taught at this point. It is something learned and reinforced during childhood. You either have it or you don't by the time you are twenty-one.

What you can do, and should do, is ask lots of questions if something doesn't seem quite right to you. Keep asking questions until you can square it in your mind. Remember, if it sounds too good to be true, it probably is.

Some things may be in a gray area. For example, it is common to have one set of forecasts for investors and another set for internal use to run the business. That may not be unethical—only you can decide if you feel comfortable with this practice.

Ask questions and trust your gut.

STAGE 5:

The Reinvention Phase

Mind-Set

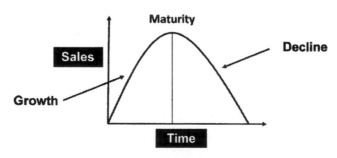

| Mind-Set | Marketing | Money | Management |

> *I'll be back in the high life again.*
> *All the doors I closed one time will open up again.*
> *I'll be back in the high life again.*
> *All the eyes that watched me once will smile*
> *and take me in.*
>
> **Back in the High Life Again**
> Written by Steve Winwood and Will Jennings

Product Life Cycle

It is important to understand that every new product and service has a product life cycle (PLC).

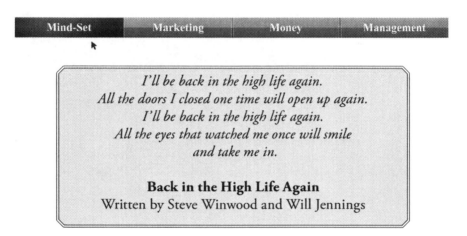

When you're at the beginning of a new product launch, it is impossible to know how quickly you'll move up the curve and how and when the curve will start to decline. Rest assured that it's not a question of *if* it will happen, but *when* it will happen. It can be an immediate decline (e.g. a fad children's toy) or a slow decline over years (e.g. replacing large, gas-guzzling cars with fuel-efficient cars).

PLCs are becoming shorter and shorter as new technologies are being introduced at a more rapid rate and are more disruptive. Once a new generation of a technology is introduced, the demand for the previous generation begins to decline rapidly and prices must be reduced. Recent examples would be iPhone and iPad—look at what they did to cell-phone demand.

Outsourcing and globalization can also accelerate PLCs. Because the decline can happen very quickly, every SFE (self-funded entrepreneur) needs to be ahead of the curve. You need to be ready to reinvent your company *in advance of the decline*. With a strategy in place, you can begin the implementation of your strategy before things fall apart.

Reinvention can create a dramatic change to your business or can be a series of smaller, incremental changes. Reinvention doesn't mean going in an entirely different direction; it can mean tweaking your current product or service to meet the changing needs of your marketplace.

Obsolete Your Own Product

You want to avoid a situation where a competitor makes your product or service obsolete. You want to obsolete your own product—meaning you want to introduce the next version of your product or service before one of your competitors does. Picture these overlapping or waterfall PLCs below:

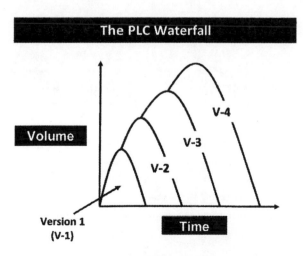

133

As you're launching Version 1 of your product or service, it's difficult if not impossible to see what Version 2 might look like. At a certain point, however, you'll need to get started developing/building/buying/creating Version 2. This will depend on the lead time to complete this task (a.k.a. time to market). It should be noted that Version 2 could be an extension of Version 1 and not necessarily an entirely new product built from the ground up.

> ## Take-Away #46
>
> Obsolete your own product or service before someone else does.

In our case, there were four major disruptive technology shifts that we had to deal with. A disruptive technology has a serious impact on the status quo and changes the way people have been dealing with a process or task. The term *disruptive* can have a negative connotation; however, these dramatic shifts can create tremendous opportunities if properly anticipated.

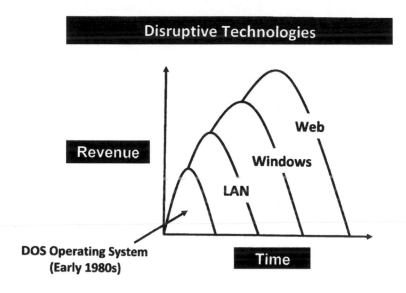

We introduced our Windows software at an industry trade show and caught our competitors flatfooted. They didn't have a Windows version of their purchasing software, and they scrambled for the next several years to catch up. Of course, the Windows version had an adverse effect on our DOS product, but in total, our revenues were up. We increased our market share and became the leader in our niche.

Making the Right Choice (and Avoiding Big Mistakes)

We were very fortunate not to have "bet on the wrong horse" during over twenty-eight years in the software business. Placing a big bet on the wrong technology can be catastrophic for a small to midsize software company.

During that time, we did place big bets on the future of DOS, LAN (local area networks), Windows, and the web. By "big bet," I mean we developed a new version of the software from the ground up to take advantage of those new operating systems and user interfaces. In retrospect, we made good choices, but at the time, no one knew for sure which technologies would prevail.

Technology platforms that received a lot of attention and buzz but never had a major impact in our market were:

- Apple's Macintosh (Hardware and OS)
- IBM's OS/2 Operating System
- IBM's PS/2 Computer
- Unix (for PCs)
- Open Source Computing
- ASP (Application Service Provider)
- Linux
- AS/400 Computers

Fortunately, we decided not to develop for any of these environments. Some were very tempting. We had received inquiries from prospects on all of these but did not pursue these opportunities. Some prospects told us their companies would be standardizing on these technologies. We were tempted but never went in those directions.

Why? First, we wanted to focus on those technologies we strongly believed in. Second, we concentrated our thinking on the ultimate end-user (customer). If the customer could do a job better and/or more easily, we carefully considered the new technology. If the end-user could not become more productive, we passed.

For example, using a mouse and a GUI (graphical user interface) could potentially make application software easier to use. Web technologies were also "game changers" because of the UI (e.g. hyperlinks) and the adoption of a "thin client" that allowed the software to reside on the server and not on each workstation. This allowed a larger number of people to use our software. You need to do your homework and then rely on your own vision and beliefs. Sometimes your strategies won't be popular with your customers or employees in the short term.

Another example is when I decided to pursue the creation of an Internet platform for our product (1996). All but two of our team thought I had lost my mind. It was obvious to them at the time that the future was Microsoft Windows and that no one would ever want to use the web for serious business applications.

Not only did 95 percent of my own company think I was nuts, but not one customer or prospect had ever asked us for a web-based automated purchasing system that incorporated catalogs, shopping carts, etc. Of course, today these applications are commonplace, but not in 1996!

Take-Away #47

The definition of an entrepreneur is someone who can create a product or service that no one knows they'll want or need.

Ultimately, these decisions helped us double the size of our company and increase our free cash flow by over a million dollars a year. This reinvention was critical to our long-term success and viability.

Focus on how the customer will benefit from your new generation of products. You need to ignore the "cool" factor with new technology and ask how it will benefit the end-user or customer. This isn't just true in the software business—it applies to all industries.

Walking the Tightrope

When you introduce your new generation, it must be done in such a way that you don't kill off your previous generation too soon. You don't want sales and maintenance to dry up overnight as everyone starts considering your new generation.

Osborne Computer released the first truly portable computer in 1981. Osborne was so pumped about their upcoming generation computer that they promoted it too strongly nine months before it was to be available. People stopped buying their current product in anticipation of getting the new and better system. Osborne had to declare bankruptcy in 1983.

A well thought-out plan must be devised that gives current customers the incentive to keep paying you while they're evaluating your new offering.

New customers should be allowed to buy the previous generation for a defined period of time with an incentive to migrate to the next generation whenever they're ready.

We made each of our four major migrations while increasing overall revenues and profits. It can be tricky. Walk the tightrope and you can become a bigger, better company.

Planned Obsolescence

Speaking of shooting oneself in the foot, one transition that could have gone better involved Y2K (the year 2000). The media had published many stories about how existing software wouldn't be able to handle years starting with 2XXX. The stories all said that current software was programmed in such a way that it couldn't handle any year after 1999.

It would have been the perfect time to get everyone to upgrade to our Windows or web products. However, a customer discovered that our DOS software handled the year 2000 perfectly. That killed our upgrade cycle for about a year. Fortunately, enough new customers bought our Windows product (that was clearly Y2K compliant) because their internally developed products couldn't handle Y2K.

If I could do it all over again, I would not have incorporated the Y2K feature in our DOS product, something that we had unknowingly done several years before. This is an example of a decision made by a well-intentioned technical person without marketing input.

Leverage Customer Experiences

Regardless of the merits of the new technology, make sure you take advantage of all the user/customer knowledge when building your new and improved product. It is difficult, if not impossible, to exclude a feature or function that you offered in previous versions. You've got to add new features while including the old capabilities.

This is the perfect time to include many of the improvements your customers have been asking for. It's a great time to shore up your weaknesses and come out a stronger company.

Take-Away #48

If it's not broken, fix it anyway. Always be working on your next generation.

STAGE 5:

The Reinvention Phase

Marketing

| Mind-Set | Marketing | Money | Management |

Changing Company or Product Names

There may be a point in the business life cycle where you'll think about changing your company name. This might be when a hot new disruptive technology is changing everything about your industry.

When Internet applications became popular, we made a decision to change our name from American Tech, Inc., to PurchasingNet, Inc. We also were moving outside the United States and were advised that a more global-sounding company name would play better.

This also gave us an opportunity to change our product name from P.O. Writer Plus to PurchasingNet. This simplified our branding challenge in that we could promote just one brand (PurchasingNet) instead of two (P.O. Writer Plus and American Tech). Of course, we made sure the Internet domain name was available before making the change. We selected *www.PurchasingNet.com* (not *www.Purchasing.net*) for our domain name. We felt like a .com extension would be more mainstream than .net.

A couple of thoughts about our name change. First, it was much more expensive than we originally thought. Signage, business cards, stationery, trade-show booths, marketing promotional items, and contracts were all affected by the change. It cost over $200,000 to make the change, so make sure there's a compelling reason to do so.

Additionally, there were hidden costs associated with the large number of form letters, proposals, and sales-support materials that included the old company logo and name. These documents needed to be changed by employees, as they were used after the name change became effective.

We later added a payables product to our product line, and having the name PurchasingNet, Inc. probably confused the marketplace. If I had to do it all over again, I might have selected the name PNet ... the P standing for purchasing, payables, etc. In fact, PNet is what all of our customers called us and our product. It just happened naturally. I wish we had figured this out before we changed our name.

The Thirty-Second Elevator Pitch

Imagine getting on an elevator with someone who might buy your product or service. You both get on in the lobby and are going to the fifteenth floor. The person asks you what you do, and you have thirty seconds to explain your business and generate some interest.

Here is an actual thirty-second elevator pitch that was written after we introduce PNet ePayables and attended an IAPP (International Accounts Payable Professionals) conference.

Thirty-Second Elevator Pitch for Controllers

PNet ePayables software helps midsize to large companies streamline the invoice-approval process for both PO invoices and non-PO invoices. It reduces invoice processing costs by $5 to $10 per invoice by reducing AP manpower, eliminating duplicate payments, and maximizing prompt payment discounts.

Our PNet eProcurement software eliminates maverick buying and provides audit trails and the internal controls needed to comply with Sarbanes Oxley.

PurchasingNet, Inc. has over 1,400 customers and has been profitable fifteen of the last seventeen years.

Pricing Models

Every industry changes its pricing model. Software, for example, has been changing from a one-time, upfront license fee with annual maintenance contracts to monthly subscription fees, which are much simpler and easy to understand.

As we added more modules to our product line, our pricing became much too complicated. It was taking hours for our sales reps to generate a quote and explain it to our prospects and customers. This was causing people to think we were becoming difficult to work with.

The other pricing trend in many industries is to move toward a recurring-revenue model. Companies with a higher percentage of recurring revenue are more valuable. Potential investors or buyers place higher multiples on predictable, ongoing revenue.

Don't be afraid to give some products or services away in return for recurring revenue that can last forever. This is especially smart when the out-of-pocket cost is very small for what you are giving away.

We also put more emphasis on multiple-year contracts with our customers. Many software companies sell a subscription-based product or service with a three- or five-year agreement. We adopted this approach, and it helped increase our recurring revenue and make us a more valuable company.

Creating More Value for Customers

The reinvention phase is a great time to think about introducing new products and services to help customers receive more value from their relationship with you.

How can you help customers get more out of their current investment with you? Can you help them increase their return on investment?

Can you offer a consulting or training service that can help your customers use your product or service more effectively? This is a great way to increase customer satisfaction and sales revenue at the same time.

Customer-Loyalty Programs

For businesses selling to consumers, consider creating a customer-loyalty program to provide incentives to buy more from you. This can be done through a point system (like charge cards use) or by giving a free product, service, or credit for every X number of times the customer buys from you.

These are very effective ways to increase value to your customers and keep them coming back. The more competitive your market is, the more you need to do this to differentiate yourself.

Make sure to keep these programs simple and easy to administer. They should be simple for the customer *and* simple for you to administer and maintain.

These programs sometimes take the form of tiered pricing, with increased discounts every time a customer orders from you.

Keep them coming back! As previously discussed, it is seven times more expensive to sell to a new customer than to sell to an existing customer.

Getting Input from Customers

Make sure to include your best customers in your reinvention process. They are a very valuable source of ideas. I used selected customers as a sounding board for new ideas.

This is a bit of a tricky area. On the one hand, you're opening yourself up to whining about the little things they don't like. On the other hand, you need to continually focus on adding value to the customer experience.

My advice: select customers who are capable of seeing the big picture, not customers who nitpick.

Stage 5:

The Reinvention Phase

Money

Building a Cushion

You never know exactly when you'll need to reinvent your business. Ideally, you'll be able to do it on your own terms, but sometimes you won't. It may be in response to a competitive threat or a poor business climate.

Reinvention is expensive but necessary for the long-term survival of any business. The funds to support this initiative need to come from the company treasury, your personal savings, or a bank line of credit.

Keep in mind that the banks view a line of credit as temporary (not permanent) financing. They'll expect you to "clean it up" or pay down the line every twelve months. If you can't do this or if you'll need the line a bit longer, make sure to communicate with the banker.

When we reinvented ourselves as a web-based software company, it cost us over a million dollars over a two-year period. It broke down as follows:

Name Change	$200K
Developing Web Products	$600K
Marketing	$200K
	$1,000K

This equated to about a 20 percent increase in annual operating expenses for two years. We didn't capitalize our development (we expensed it), so there was a million-dollar hit to our income statement and cash flow.

Financial Impact of Reinventing Yourself

On the revenue side, try to figure out if the new, enhanced product or service will cannibalize existing business or add to your total revenue. Perhaps it will do both.

The ideal reinvention results in products or services that can increase your market share *and* be "sold" back to your current customers as an upgrade.

Fortunately, each of our reinventions allowed us to expand our market for new customers and generate incremental revenue by selling back to our installed base as an add-on or upgrade.

One of the things a small company has to avoid is announcing the next generation too soon. You may feel like you want to tell everyone about the great new generation you are working on, but if word gets out, prospects won't buy your current product. They'll wait until the new product is available before buying anything from you. You would be well-advised to wait until the new product is physically available and ready to ship before announcing your new generation.

This is one area where your big competitors have a decided advantage over you. They can announce their next generation a year or more in advance and freeze the entire marketplace. Everyone will wait to see what the new generation will look like before buying *anything*—yours or theirs.

If you can beat your competitors to the punch, you can generate some buzz and fuel your growth engine before you are put on the defensive. Proactive reinvention will keep you in the driver's seat.

Patents

The patent system was put in place to protect inventors of new, unique, and useful ideas from competitors copying them.

Patents are supposed to level the playing field and protect inventors. At one point in the evolution of the patent system, this worked nicely.

Then, in the 1990s, software and intellectual property became eligible for patent protection. Business methods could also be patented. These two changes opened the floodgates for thousands upon thousands of new patents.

It is also interesting to note that ideas can be patented. They don't necessarily have to be real products, actual software, or efficient methods of doing things.

And now for the unintended consequences—the patent system is creating additional expenses and "headwinds" for the SFE. It is also making innovation more difficult. Here are some of the reasons why:

- Filing a patent and going through the initial review process is currently taking three-and-a-half years. It can be an additional two years to get the patent approved.
- The cost to develop and submit a patent can be many thousands of dollars—even if you write it up yourself.
- Big companies like Microsoft have turned into "patent machines," submitting thousands of patents every year.
- With the addition of business methods to the patent process, many ridiculous patents ("obvious" in patent lingo) have been submitted and in some cases approved for process—like applying a stamp to an envelope, filing a document, approving a document, filling out a request form.
- In a lawsuit, the patent holder wins 94 percent of the cases, regardless of who may be right or wrong. Jurors believe the PTO (Patent and Trademark Office) would never have awarded a patent in the first place unless the applicant was deserving of it.
- Some companies buy other companies with significant patent portfolios for the sole purpose of initiating patent-infringement litigation. These are known as "patent trolls."

Patent-infringement can be settled out of court by licensing the technology or business method in question. Infringement judgments often exceed $100 million. Accordingly, companies will spend millions of dollars in litigation to win a case or keep from losing one.

Our company was once a "prior art" witness in a patent infringement case. The defendant spent over $10 million in legal fees, and the plaintiff spent over $5 million bringing the case. The case ended in a hung jury, and the defendant ultimately paid $17 million to settle the case and avoid the retrial. Laurene testified for four hours in federal court in Virginia.

The irony is that our company actually developed the original technology long before software companies could even apply for a patent! That's why we were called to testify in the case.

The post mortem to this case: The PTO invalidated the patent after the $17 million settlement. The owner of the patent contested this decision and is therefore allowed to continue to sue companies for patent infringement during the reexamination process. During this period, several of our competitors wrote checks to the patent owner to license their technology instead of spending funds to fight an expensive battle where the deck is overwhelmingly stacked against you. For a large company, it's a drop in the bucket. For an SFE, it is distracting, nerve-racking, and potentially financially devastating.

I am sure there are some benefits of patent law for the SFE. I just don't know what they are. I do know that this can be a very expensive undertaking and very distracting for the SFE.

And I do know it makes some lawyers very, very wealthy. It has provided increased revenue to the US government through the PTO.

These laws need to be changed. We innovated and beat the big guys to the punch. In time, we expected the big guys to improve their offerings, and they did. It's fair competition, and it benefits the marketplace. Changing or eliminating the patent system would increase innovation.

I suppose we could have brought a lawsuit against Oracle, Microsoft, or SAP if we had patented our early ideas, but that's not why we went into business. It would have been all-consuming for *years*, and we would have lost all focus on running the business.

STAGE 5:

The Reinvention Phase

Management

Mind-Set	Marketing	Money	Management

Creating the Right Environment for Reinvention

You'd be surprised where great ideas come from. Sometimes they can be from a clerical person or the guy that performs a repetitive task on the shop floor every day. If you recognize this fact, you will create an environment in your company where people have enough confidence to approach you with an idea for how to improve the product or service.

Don't confuse this with encouraging people to whine and complain.

I had a very simple rule about people who came into my office to complain. First, they were welcomed to come in at any time. Second, if they complained about something, they had to provide me with at least one way the problem could have been avoided or solved. This process forces people to think about how to solve little problems before they become big problems.

Brainstorming

One of the great techniques for generating new ideas is brainstorming. I never believed that all-day brainstorming sessions were productive, however. A couple of hour sessions worked best for us. Any longer and we got too far off the subject, any less and we couldn't dive deep enough.

There are two different styles of brainstorming. The first is a top-down approach where someone (you?) thinks through various scenarios or alternatives and presents them to the group for discussion and feedback. The second is a more democratic method in which people just throw out ideas without first thinking them through. Every idea voiced is explored.

In our case, the top-down method was superior to the democratic method. We tended to stay more focused and brainstormed ideas that had received at least some thought and analysis before being discussed. The democratic approach often wasted time exploring impractical ideas.

We also found it very difficult to brainstorm in our offices. There were too many interruptions. We eventually moved most of our brainstorming sessions off-site.

Another type of brainstorming session was held every year at our client forum. Our customers spent about three hours talking about how we could improve our products and services. They developed a list of ideas and then voted on them so we could prioritize our subsequent development efforts.

This made our customers feel like we were listening to them (we were!) and highlighted the most popular ideas so we could get a sense of what was truly important to them. It resulted in a better product and stronger customer relationships. It should be noted that we brought several key resources from product development and engineering to the client forum so they could hear firsthand what issues were important to customers. They could also meet with clients to clarify their understanding of the problem or need.

Consultants

For the most part, consultants are worthless.

I used to be one, so I should know.

The reasons are many—not the least of which is lack of relevant experience, not having to live with the consequences of their recommendations, consistently overpromising and under-delivering, and the outrageous cost of their services.

That said, a consultant can be of some value as you try to reinvent yourself. Just make sure you *hire an individual and not a consulting company.* Also make sure you agree on deliverables and appropriate milestone payments.

We used a consultant to help us think through our reinvention as a web-based or Internet software company. We ended up becoming an enterprise software company with an average deal size that was ten to twenty times greater than our PC product.

This required dramatic changes throughout our company—R&D, Sales, Marketing, Professional Services, and Customer Support all had to be upgraded to support this major reinvention.

It helped to have someone from outside the company give us input to help guide us through this transition. At the very least, we had a good sounding board who gave us his honest opinion whenever we needed it.

The consultant helped us create a vision for the future that guided us through the next twelve years. Our $25,000 investment in the right consultant paid many dividends.

Board of Advisors

A formal or informal board of advisors can act as a sounding board during your reinvention initiatives. They can bring a different perspective on your vision and help you evaluate various scenarios you may be considering.

The board should be made up of people you know and trust. They should be able to give you advice on how you can improve *your* business, not theirs. Make sure there are no built-in biases on your board. Make sure you have each of the Four M's represented.

There's no need to have regularly scheduled meetings, but you should be able to call or e-mail board members on an as-needed basis. Of course, as an SFE, you would like not to pay them for their services. For those not billing for their time, make sure to take them out to lunch or dinner periodically to show your appreciation for their guidance.

Frankly, I wish I'd had a more formal board of advisors with more participants. It could have relieved some of the pressure on me and helped us consider other alternatives as the company evolved.

Management Changes

Now is a good time to make changes in your management team. As you go through the reinvention process, you will be able to sense that certain individuals aren't capable of helping the company move to the next level.

Some of your managers may not feel comfortable with the direction you are heading. Some will leave of their own accord. Some may require termination. Some people just hate change of any kind.

Still others will be supportive and able to continue to contribute to the company's success. Others are willing to step up but will need some help to do so. These folks deserve your help—as long as they're willing to make the commitment to do whatever's necessary to remain a member of the team.

At this stage, negativity among employees can spread like a cancer. When we decided to make the move to a web-based platform for our product, we lost about 40 percent of our team. This was a combination of people leaving on their own and terminations we initiated. There was some short-term pain, but within a year we were stronger than ever. Our laggards were gone, and we had hired some stronger team members to help us get to the next level.

Lifetime Learning

Lifetime learning is critical to reinvention. Without making the effort and putting in the time, you won't be capable of knowing where to take the company next.

"Constant change is here to stay." Someone told me this early in my entrepreneurial career, and truer words have never been spoken.

Read and think. Talk to others. Watch TV. Go online. Go back to school. Get some training. Attend a seminar. There are many cost-effective ways to learn. But you must be willing to put in the time to stay ahead of the curve. Plan to devote at least two or three hours a day, every day, to learning and growing.

Take-Away #49

If you don't learn something new every day, you aren't trying hard enough.

Hedging Your Bets

You may think you've reinvented your company and are now ready to place a big bet on your new direction.

Don't bet the ranch.

Many times, new ideas just don't work as anticipated in the marketplace. It's good to get real-world market confirmation before placing a large bet on a new idea. At this stage, you have too much to lose if your idea flops.

Get a few customer orders or at least firm verbal commitments from customers you trust before investing a significant amount in your new direction.

An example of this was a product we developed and named EAST (equipment and service tracking). EAST was going to take us in a new direction (pun intended). It would allow companies to track all of their PCs, networks, furniture, etc. This was a frequently expressed need in the marketplace.

We brought this product to market, and it flopped. We booked no orders whatsoever. Why? We weren't exactly sure. It could have been that people expected the software to handle depreciation like a fixed-assets system. More likely, it was a case where people thought it was a good idea but weren't willing to pay for it. They thought they could handle it themselves using spreadsheets.

Regardless, the market voted with its feet. Fortunately, we had only invested about $50K developing the product and bringing it to market.

We dropped the product after six months. Sometimes it's best to cut your losses and move on.

STAGE 6:

Decline (and Cost-Cutting)
Mind-Set

> *I walk a lonely road*
> *The only one that I have ever known*
> *Don't know where it goes*
> *But it's home to me and I walk alone.*
>
> **Boulevard of Broken Dreams**
> Written by Michael Pritchard, Frank E.
> Wright, and Billie Joe Armstrong

My eleven-year corporate career had prepared me well for cost-cutting. But no matter how prepared you are, cost-cutting usually adversely affects people's lives and isn't fun for you or your employees.

As the ultimate decision-maker on cost-cutting, you walk a lonely road. You will spend countless hours trying to figure out how to cut costs without losing business and without hurting your employees.

Temporary or Permanent Decline?

Before taking any action whatsoever, you need to try to figure out what is causing your decline in business. There are generally seven causes for decline:

1. External Events
2. Economic Reasons
3. Industry Trends
4. Seasonal Influences
5. "Man-Made" Boom/Bust Cycle
6. Internal Process Breakdown
7. Product Life-Cycle Decline

Decline Examples

External Events: Examples of this are the stock-market crash of 1987; the attacks of September 11, 2001; oil spills; and weather events. These are mostly one-time events that are difficult, if not impossible, to anticipate.

Economic Reasons: This would include recessions and depressions, whether global or local. Examples of this are the financial meltdown and Great Recession of 2008–2010.

Industry Trends: This could be caused by the impact of globalization, outsourcing, or new disruptive technologies, such as the Internet or mobile phones. It could also be caused by the introduction of a significant new competitor(s).

Seasonal Influences: Historically, summer months are very slow for business. In our business, we were personally depressed every August because sales were almost nonexistent in July or August.

"Man-Made" Boom/Bust Cycles: Y2K was a good example of this. Demand for many products increased prior to December 31, 1999, and declined afterward.

Internal Processes: Decline can be caused by changes within your company. Changes in any of the Four M's can have an adverse effect on business. These changes could result in a string of competitive losses.

Product Life Cycle: Decline could be caused by being on the downside of the life cycle.

Once you determine the cause of the decline, you need to answer the following question: "Is this decline permanent or temporary?" The answer to this question will help guide you in your cost-reduction efforts.

For example, let's say you believe that your decline in sales is being caused by a recession that you believe will end within a year (the typical recession lasts nine to eighteen months). In this case, you may want to avoid layoffs and look to other areas for cost reductions. The cost of laying people off and rehiring in a year may exceed the cost reduction potential of the layoff.

Conversely, if you believe a decline is being caused by industry trends that will be long-lasting or permanent, layoffs need to be made quickly. The longer you wait, the worse it will be. While you wait, morale will deteriorate and cost reductions won't be as significant. Ultimately, you'll have to lay off more people to make up for it.

For example, the introduction of web-based technologies in the software industry caused a decline of Windows-based software applications. This was a megatrend (a term used by John Naisbitt in his bestseller *Megatrends*) that couldn't be ignored. It allowed many Internet companies to grow and flourish while Windows-centric companies were forced to lay off many employees.

Take-Away #50

You can't fight a megatrend.

That's why it's important to continually learn about your industry and constantly reevaluate trends to determine if they are fads that will pass or megatrends that will have a lasting impact on your business.

A temporary decline in business is manageable. You do a little belt-tightening, hope that your analysis has been correct, and live to play another day.

Permanent or long-term decline is another story. It can be very painful. You feel like everybody has turned against you at the same time. You feel like your head is in a vise. As someone once said, "It feels like you're in the movie *Groundhog Day*," the movie starring Bill Murray. It's the same negative things happening over and over. You feel like you've lost all control and things are hopeless.

There is no time to waste once you've concluded the decline is permanent.

Ten Tips for Dealing with a Long-Term or Permanent Decline

1. Don't live in the past. Past performance doesn't guarantee future success. Things don't always return to the good old days.
2. Don't rest on your laurels. Always be anticipating and reinventing.
3. Once you become convinced of a long-term issue, move quickly to adjust to your new world. Don't be a "deer in the headlights."
4. Despite rapid decision-making, it takes some time to work through issues. People would like to see immediate solutions, but dealing with a decline takes patience. Try to maintain your sanity until you right the ship.

5. Take one day at a time. Don't try to predict when things will get better.
6. Don't worry about what you can't control.
7. Compartmentalize your life so the pressure of dealing with a decline doesn't spill over to your personal life.
8. Take care of yourself by exercising more and drinking less.
9. Just think of how much stronger your company will be when you come out the other end.
10. Make sure you have saved enough money to weather the storm. That's what's meant by "saving for a rainy day."

Stage 6:

Decline (and Cost-Cutting)
Marketing

Getting Creative

Even though you may be in a decline, don't lose sight of the fundamentals of how to improve cash flow. That means not only cutting costs but also increasing revenues. Success may mean slowing the rate of your revenue decline.

The most important thing to do is focus on your existing customers. For the time being, don't be concerned about adding new customers. Of course, you won't turn away a new customer, but you can't "chase rabbits," either.

As previously discussed, it is far more cost-effective to sell to an existing customer than to find a new one. The question you need to ask yourself is, "How can I help my existing customers get more benefit and value from my products or services?"

Here are some techniques to consider when in a declining period:
- Discounts for purchases made before a certain date
- Customer-loyalty programs
- Gift certificates or gift cards
- Prompt-payment discounts
- Bundling—including additional products and services in each sale
- Increase annual subscription costs by including more value
- Increased subscription term in return for a discount (e.g. two years, three years, five years)

155

- Extended warranties and guarantees
- Money-back guarantees
- Thirty-day free trial
- E-mail or phone campaign to current customers
- Flexible pricing plans (lease, buy, subscribe)
- Platinum, gold, and silver service plans
- Emphasis on account management and increase in customer contacts
- New products and services that you have already provided to other customers

Not all of these will apply to every business, but they are all worthy of consideration.

Some may seem a little hokey, but they work! Don't let customers know you are in decline. If you do, it can become a self-fulfilling prophecy because no one wants to buy from a declining business. When asked, simply say business is strong.

Don't give any hint of being needy or desperate. Just act like you don't need the sale. As the old TV commercial says, "Never let them see you sweat." Customers are like dogs—they can sense it if you're scared.

Increasing Recurring Revenue

This is a great time to offer prepaid maintenance plans to current customers. You can also offer discounts for committing to (or paying for) multiple-year maintenance plans.

We also introduced two different maintenance plans—one basic and one enhanced—and sold many upgrades to our customer base. This helped us survive and thrive during the period of 2001–2003 ... a very tough time for all businesses.

New Customers

One of the very successful strategies we developed happened during a period of decline after September 11, 2001. We decided to focus all of our marketing efforts on vertical markets.

We started to realize that we couldn't successfully market our software to every midsize and large company in the United States. We simply didn't have the resources to compete with the big boys on every opportunity. We had to pick our battles.

We analyzed the vertical markets where we had been successful and determined that since we had sold our software to seven of the largest law firms in the world, we would concentrate on the law-firm vertical market. We had virtually no competition in this market, and law firms tend to be a "me too" industry. Law firms always ask, "What other law firms are using your software?" Once they heard the names of the law firms, they became very comfortable with us and our product.

We tailored our marketing and sales efforts to the legal market. Our salespeople learned the "language" of a large law firm and could illustrate how our software could help them increase their PPP (profit per partner).

We also identified the financial-services market as a good one for us. We already had a number of case studies describing how banks, brokerages, and mortgage companies had saved millions of dollars by using our products.

We concentrated on these two verticals, and reaped lower marketing costs and increased company sales during a "nuclear winter" for the software industry.

Of course, we would still take leads and sales that came in from other industries. We just didn't spend much money to get the leads or close deals in industries other than legal and financial services.

Product Development

A period of temporary decline is a great time to put your people to work creating new and improved products and services.

Rather than incurring the cost of laying off and then rehiring and retraining, utilize your current resources to improve your offerings. Think of it as making an investment in your business that will pay back many times over once the temporary decline is over. You'll be a stronger, better company when business improves.

We created an entirely new product line in 2002–2003 when business was very slow in the software industry. Our ePayables product suite cost us about $250K to develop, but it turned out to be one of the best investments we ever made—certainly better than investing in the stock market.

The ePayables suite allowed us to expand our market and start selling our products to the real decision-makers: controllers and CFs of midsize to large companies.

The payback was significant. We generated an additional $4 million in revenue and $1 million in net income. Hard to beat that return on investment!

Stage 6:

Decline (and Cost-Cutting)

Money

On the revenue side, make every attempt to increase cash flow by offering incentives for prompt or early payments. In a declining environment, it's worth giving up a few percentage points to ensure early payment.

Now is a great time to offer both existing customers and prospects a discount if they buy before a certain date. The discount/deadline strategy will accelerate some orders, but there can be a "valley" after the deadline has passed. Your hope, of course, is that you improve cash flow during the tough times and that business will improve in the not-too-distant future.

Staff Reductions

In most businesses, manpower expenses are the major element of the annual "budget." I use the word "budget" in quotes because budgets can be virtually worthless if they can't keep up with changing business conditions. Budgets are typically obsolete the day after they are approved. Budgets can't keep up in a period of decline.

You've got to react to the decline after you've analyzed the situation and made an educated guess on the projected duration of the decline, regardless of when the budget was approved and how much you have left to spend.

One technique that can be used is the GE "forced ranking" technique. GE developed a process of ranking all employees in each job classification based on performance and laying off the bottom 10 percent every year. This can be done in good years and bad years, and serves to continually prune the dead wood.

Another very basic cost-cutting technique is to tell all managers they must cut their expenditures by X percent per year. This is a useful approach when every department feels like it's overworked and the other guy should be doing the cutting. This technique is a bit simplistic, but it will cut through the "BS" and get fast results. Recognize that you may be cutting into some muscle in certain areas and not cutting deep enough in others, but you'll get the ball rolling.

For permanent or longer-term declines, you will want to identify your core team members based on a Greenfield approach, which asks the following question: "If a new organization were to be formed, what has to be done and how would it be done?" It's a good way to take a fresh look at your company and your organization. Some people refer to this as a "clean sheet of paper" approach. It asks the question, "How would you redesign the business if you were starting from scratch?" This exercise helps determine minimum manpower levels required.

Temporary Manpower Reductions

Before you go through the painful process of laying off people, evaluate several other cost-reduction alternatives.

The first alternative to consider is a salary-reduction program in which everyone takes a pay reduction of X percent for Y months. To offset the pain, you can offer additional vacation time to everyone. So, for example, if everyone has to take a 5 percent pay cut, that would equate to twelve work days of pay each year. You can offer twelve days of "unpaid vacation" in return for the 5 percent reduction. We did this several times during temporary declines, and it was very well-received by most employees.

You could be selective in who participates, but an "everybody shares the pain" approach will have the best impact on employee morale.

Travel Expenses

Travel is one of the first things to go in a downturn. By using web-based tools like WebEx, Skype, and GoToMeeting, you can help soften the blow of reduced travel and stay in touch with your prospects and customers.

Marketing Expenses

Marketing expenses are the second thing to go. It is very easy to reduce advertising, events, promotional activities, and so on.

For example, in 2001, we reduced public-relations projects, print advertising, direct mail, brochures, and other marketing expenses, saving $400K per year. This represented about 10 percent of our total company expenditures. It resulted in an 80 percent reduction in marketing expenditures.

The argument for reducing marketing expenses in bad times is that it's very difficult to measure the ROI of any marketing program, and few people would buy your product regardless of the marketing investment.

Rent Reduction

Even though you may have signed a five-year lease on rental space, you can still negotiate lower monthly rent by giving back some of the space you no longer need.

Another possibility is to offer to extend the term of your current lease in exchange for lower monthly rent. Many landlords value a lease extension and are willing to negotiate lower rents in exchange for predictability.

A third technique is to sublet some of your space (check your lease agreement first). If you go this route, make sure you don't rent to a disruptive person or company. They should be quiet, not require any attention from you, and not generate lots of foot traffic through the space (unless you want it). The last thing you want is to be distracted by a temporary tenant during a tough economic time.

During one decline, we found a temporary tenant that was a start-up. The owners wanted a prestigious address but didn't need access to the space until after business hours. They were also willing to use a side stairway, which allowed us to give them a private space by simply locking two doors and installing a separate alarm system for their protection and ours. They paid $2,000 a month, which was a bargain for them and positive cash flow for us.

On another occasion, we reduced our rent by 33 percent by using all of these techniques. We gave back space we no longer needed, we extended our lease by two years, and we sublet a small portion of our space. We saved over $10,000 a month by taking these steps.

If you're not sure how to go about this, a commercial real-estate consultant can help.

Renegotiate with Suppliers

You don't have a lot of time to select new suppliers, but it may be worth spending a few hours to renegotiate prices and terms with your current suppliers.

Tell your high-volume suppliers that you will be sending a list of their products or services out for bid, and that you will be getting bids from two to four new suppliers (their competitors). Of course, you will also include them in the bidding process.

About two weeks later, give your current supplier a list of all the items you buy from them, and tell them that if they would like, they can give you a "preemptive bid," avoid the formal sourcing process, and save everyone some time. They can keep your business if their prices are more competitive.

Explain that if their current prices are reduced by X percent, you will continue to buy from them for the next twelve months. In return, you will put your sourcing efforts on hold during this period. Their competitors won't get a chance to steal their customer.

You will be surprised how much money you can save by using this approach. The only time required is the time to identify a few of your supplier's competitors and generate a list of what you buy from your supplier (include quantities and current prices if you can).

This approach will typically generate a 5 percent to 15 percent cost reduction. While you're at it, you can negotiate more favorable payment terms that give you more time to pay and/or give you prompt payment discounts that can save you another 1 to 3 percent.

Placing a Value on Your Time

This renegotiating exercise will consume several hours of your time. Let's say you value your time at $100 per hour, and this task will take four hours. Let's say you spend $20,000 a year with a given supplier.

If it costs you $400 (your time), but you can save 10 percent x $20,000, that effort results in a five-fold payback.

Try getting a "five-bagger" in the stock market! This negotiating exercise is a no-brainer. It is well worth your time.

Negotiate with Your Banker

During a decline, it is always a good idea to renegotiate with your banker to get such advantages as lower interest rates, reduced collateral requirements, and more favorable loan covenants.

You can hire a company or individual to help you identify a new bank for you and negotiate favorable terms on your behalf.

We secured a low-interest $1.5 million line of credit with a personal guarantee (with minimal collateral) and favorable loan covenants for a onetime fee of $20,000. This investment was well worth it. It saved us about $30,000 per year in interest costs.

Any initiative that has a payback period of less than one year should move to the top of your to-do list.

Employee Benefits

During a prolonged decline, it is not unusual to reduce employee benefits. Some of the actions we took included:

- Stopped matching employee contributions to 401(k)s
- Stopped contributing to company profit-sharing plan
- Increased employee contribution for health insurance from 20 percent to 27 percent
- Reduced or eliminated employee perks (water cooler, snacks, etc.)

People are typically not happy with these changes. One of our top salespeople understood why we made these changes—except for the water cooler (which he used frequently). He later left the company and cited the lack of a water cooler as the main reason for leaving!

It wasn't really the lack of the water cooler; he just thought that a company that would take a water cooler away was in real trouble. He didn't realize it represented a savings of $3,000 per year. People just don't understand how much small things cost when *they* aren't paying the bills.

Any changes to benefits are very emotional. Make sure you communicate early and often with your employees during this stressful time.

Our Cost Reduction Scorecard

Some of our ongoing cost reductions included:

Source	Annual Savings
Manpower	$1,000K
Print Advertising	$200K
Other Marketing	$200K
Travel	$50K
Shut Down Hosting Product	$80K
401(k) Matching	$20K
Interest Expenses	$20K
Rent	$100K
Search-Engine Marketing	$60K
Miscellaneous Supplier Savings	$30K
Total Annual Savings:	**$1,760K**
One-Time Savings	
Shut Down Singapore Joint Venture	$300K
10 Percent Salary Cut for One Year	$60K
Executives' Salary Reduction	$80K
Total Savings:	**$440K**

The end result of these cuts is that we maintained profitability when business declined. For example, in 2009, we managed to achieve positive cash flow of $1,000,000 despite a 25 percent reduction in revenues over a two-year period.

Some might think we cut too much, and we were being greedy. This certainly was not the case.

Many of our prospects and customers required an annual financial review of all of their suppliers. It was imperative that our balance sheet and income statement looked strong. It would have been nice to not cut employees, but if you can't win new business or keep existing accounts, then it's all for nothing. These are tough choices for the SFE.

STAGE 6:

Decline (and Cost-Cutting)

Management

Mind-Set	Marketing	Money	Management

Core People

Layoffs are very painful. Losing a job can be devastating to employees and their families.

It is also a difficult time for the SFE. Layoffs are not taken lightly. I spent countless hours analyzing my staff trying to figure out how many people to lay off and who should be laid off.

Every time I thought I had the answer, I would think about it again ... and again ... and again.

One of the first steps is to figure out who is in your core group. These are the employees whom you would never want to lose under any circumstances. In our case, we had about 50 percent of our employees that we considered core and crucial to our success.

Once you make this determination, communicate with all of your core people. Let them know that their jobs are safe, and they are valued employees. Let them know that there may be layoffs in the future, but they don't have to worry about them—their jobs are safe.

Forced Ranking: The Bottom 10 Percent

The bottom 10 percent (based on performance and value to the company) should be easy to identify.

To avoid any potential legal issues, make sure you have documentation to back up the fact that these are your poorest performers. This should be in the form of substandard performance reviews, warning letters in the HR file, etc. These will be needed to counter any discrimination claims.

If you don't have this kind of documented support for your position, you may have to simply use the "last hired, first fired" method of laying people off. Unfortunately, this may result in losing some very talented people and retaining the weaker people.

Marginal Employees

So far, we have determined the status of 60 percent of the employees. What about the other 40 percent?

Employee Status

Core 50 percent
Marginal 40 percent
Bottom 10 percent

This is a difficult and emotional exercise.

To remove the emotion, you'll need to develop parameters to evaluate the employees in the marginal group. I rated each marginal employee on a scale of 1 to 10 in the following areas:

1. Impact on our business in the next six months (1 = Least Impact)
2. Compensation relief   (1 = Most Relief)
3. Cost to rehire/retrain   (1 = Lowest Cost)

The results were as follows:

Employee	Position	A	B	C	Total
1	Administrative Assistant	2	7	2	11
2	Sales Manager	6	1	9	16
3	Business Development	5	5	3	13
4	Programmer 1	7	3	5	15
5	Consultant 1	5	5	6	16
6	Consultant 2	5	4	7	16
7	Help Desk	5	8	5	18
8	IT Support	3	9	4	16
9	Programmer 2	4	7	8	19
10	Programmer 3	4	7	8	19

We ended up having to lay off three people from the marginal group. We followed the ratings and laid off employees 1, 3, and 4. These three had the lowest scores.

Giving a Heads-Up

We liked to give people a heads-up that they were going to be laid off. We tried to give people a six- to eight-week head start in getting a new job. The concept was that "it's easier to get a job if you have a job."

The conditions were: a) the employees had to continue doing their job during this period, and b) they couldn't tell anyone except their families. We allowed them to take some time to find a new job. Some people were simply too immature to handle this option, regardless of their actual age. When we determined that the person would not be able to emotionally handle a heads-up, this wasn't used. These were people who had a track record of not being able to keep things to themselves or people who were prone to negativity.

This worked well in all but a couple of cases. It was the most humane way to handle layoffs and soften the blow of a layoff. People will be grateful you gave them a head start.

Moving Quickly

Once your analysis is complete, move quickly and implement your plan. By waiting, you will only damage morale and decrease cash flow—both undesirable outcomes.

Tell each employee being laid off his or her fate individually and behind closed doors. Make sure you have two people with the employee. Don't terminate people one-on-one to avoid any possibility of a "he said/she said" legal issue down the road. Document the meeting immediately afterward. Do it late in the day so it has a minimal impact on everyone else. Have a box of tissues ready. Be ready for any kind of reaction (e.g. extreme anger, laughter, hysteria).

STAGE 7:

Selling the Company
Mind-Set

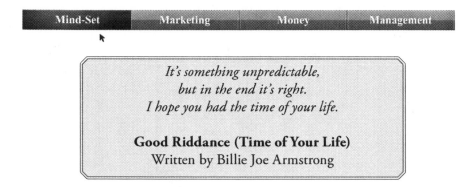

A nd we did have the time of our life. There were a few painful episodes, but we always fought our way through the tough times.

We accomplished everything we set out to do and then some. We were challenged, we made a contribution, we were fulfilled, and we (mostly) controlled our own destiny. We had fun, we created new jobs, and we made more money than we ever dreamed possible.

No regrets. I hope every SFE (self-funded entrepreneur) gets the same opportunity that we had.

M&A (Mergers and Acquisitions)

When we first started our software business, we weren't thinking about selling the business. We were thinking about surviving, making it to the break-even point, and becoming a profitable and viable organization.

We were told by some other SFEs that "the only reason to start a business is to sell the business." In fact, some very successful entrepreneurs follow that advice. We did not. In fact, we were on the other end of the spectrum and didn't even think about selling out until we had been in business fifteen years. Only then did we start preparing the business for sale. In hindsight, we should have started preparing sooner than we did.

Preparing for Sale

We were in no hurry to sell the business but thought if we got a good offer, we would give it serious consideration. Up to that point, when making a decision, we evaluated the impact on customers, employees, cash flow, etc. As you start thinking about exiting the business via a sale or merger, you need to understand the thought process of a potential acquirer. When making a decision, you need to think about how this will increase (or decrease) the value of your business in the eyes of a potential acquirer.

Value Drivers

Each industry has different value drivers.

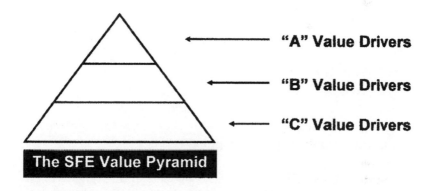

The value drivers described below and their relative importance applied to our company, PurchasingNet, Inc. The value drivers can be substantially different for different industries.

Note that some of the value drivers are *not* things you may be thinking about today. For example, you may not be concentrating on revenue growth, but you may live and die with customer satisfaction. This is not consistent with what many buyers are looking for. Growth trumps customer satisfaction in most cases.

"A" Value Drivers

- **Revenue Growth:** For most technology businesses, revenue growth is far and away the most important determinant of enterprise value. The valuation of a software business is commonly stated as a multiple of annual revenue. For example, during the Internet boom, software companies were valued at up to ten times annual revenue (or more). During the Internet bust, software values were in the one- to three-times range (or lower). Normally, revenue multiples are based on the last twelve months (LTM) or the trailing twelve months (TTM).

   Acquirers are interested in both your history and what they believe they can achieve when your company becomes part of theirs. The hope is that under their control, with their resources, they can accelerate revenue growth. As GE used to say, "1 + 1 = 3." A business that can be grown with minimal additional effort is referred to as a "highly scalable business." This is what acquirers desire.

- **Technology:** If you are utilizing the same technology as the acquirer, integrating the two companies will be easier and less costly than if the two companies use different technologies.

- **Profitability:** The importance of profitability varies depending on the overall direction of the economy. In boom times, profitability is not very important to the acquirer. In tough economic times, profitability becomes very important.

   In general, profitability and positive cash flow are important to most acquirers. They want their acquisitions to be "accretive" to earnings as quickly as possible. (Translation: they want acquisitions to increase profits, not decrease profits.)

- **Visibility:** This means more than being able to forecast revenues and net income. This means you already have actual orders and contracts for products and services that you will be providing in the future. Some refer to this as "backlog."

- **Recurring Revenue:** This means that there are actual service contracts and subscriptions with existing customers that extend into the future. This has become the second most important factor (behind growth) for most acquirers.

- **Size:** Acquirers rarely are interested in smaller companies unless there is a compelling strategic reason for a merger or acquisition. Size *does* matter. It takes an acquirer the same amount of time and effort to acquire a $2 million company as a $10 million company. In some ways, it is even easier to acquire the $10 million company because that company is likely to have better financial systems and controls than a smaller company.

"B" Value Drivers

- **Management Team:** The quality and depth of your management team is a factor in the decision to acquire. The acquirer wants to know that your company can run without you (in case you leave or get hit by a bus).

- **Customer Base:** The number of active customers and the quality of the customer base is important to many acquirers. They believe they can sell *their* products and services to your customers.

- **Unique Position in the Market:** Buyers value uniqueness. They are looking for companies that are complementary to theirs. Most acquiring companies aren't interested in companies that have overlap with their own products and services. Companies with overlap rarely get acquired; they tend to get squashed in the marketplace by big competitors.

- **Financial Processes:** There can be no doubt in the buyer's mind that you have sound financial systems and controls. Also, if the buyer uses accrual accounting, make sure you can easily present your financial statements using this method of accounting. They'll be looking at the last three years of your financials.

- **Making It Easy on the Buyer:** If buyers sense there will be lots of work and complications with the deal, they'll likely back away.

"C" Value Drivers

- **Market Size:** In addition to the current overall market size (in terms of total revenue), a buyer will want to know your market share. Very often acquirers will want to know the "addressable" market size to gauge the opportunity.

171

- **Domain Expertise:** How much do you and your teams know about your market segment? Patents can be helpful. Awards can be useful. Experience is valued.

- **Customer Satisfaction:** Every company says they have happy customers. Third-party "proof" can be useful to prove your point.

- **Partnerships:** Forming partnerships with other companies is a good way to find a potential buyer. If you've actually worked with the buying company in the past, it can lead to a transaction.

- **Culture:** If potential buying companies see you and your team as a "good fit" with their team, that can be a big positive.

Strategic versus Financial Buyers

The valuation of a company purchased for strategic reasons is significantly higher than a company purchased purely for financial reasons.

Strategic buyers are interested in plugging a hole in their product/service lineup or entering an entirely new market. They have gone through a "make versus buy" analysis and determined that there are more advantages to buying an existing company with an existing product (and hopefully some real customers) than developing the same capability themselves. In the technology industries, "time to market" is dramatically reduced by acquiring a company. This separates winners from losers in technology industries.

Financial buyers don't particularly care about your product or service, only whether it can make them money and give them a good return on investment.

The valuation scale for a software business looks something like this:

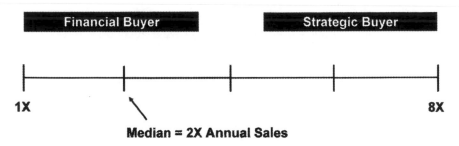

Most valuations fall somewhere in between. The median valuation (for the software industry) historically has been approximately 1.5X to 2.5X.

When to Sell

There are many factors involved in deciding when to sell your business. From a valuation standpoint, it is most advantageous to sell when you're growing and when multiple strategic buyers want to buy your business. In our case, the Internet boom of the late 1990s was one such period.

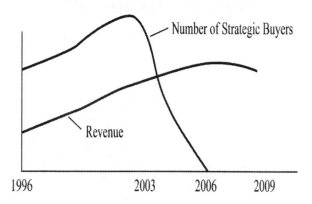

In retrospect, 2005 would have been a great time to sell. Unfortunately, you really don't know what is going on around you when you are "inside the tornado." It's only when you look back that you know when would have been the best time to sell.

Another indicator is when you start feeling surly every day or when you just want to move on and do something else. You may not maximize your valuation, but you'll maintain your sanity and remain a positive person.

After twenty-eight years, we needed to move on. We were ready for a change. I must admit, we were getting a bit surly and were running out of gas.

STAGE 7:

Selling the Company

Marketing

| Mind-Set | Marketing | Money | Management |

Do I Need Help from a Third Party?

Finding a buyer is a time-consuming endeavor.

Let me share some numbers with you. Over a twelve-year period, we contacted over five hundred companies and had about seventy-five conversations with potential buyers.

During this period, we had twenty-four very serious conversations (talked multiple times and visited at least once). Of these twenty-four, six "got to the altar" before we finally found "the one."

During this twelve-year period, I spent anywhere from 10 percent to 40 percent of my time on this initiative. At an average of 25 percent, that meant I spent three years of my life preparing, planning, and executing an acquisition. And this was using an investment banker to help us!

If I didn't use a middleman, I might have spent twice this amount of time.

How to Select a Middleman

The two most important factors in selecting a middleman are their areas of expertise and the particular individual you will be working with.

For example, if you own a software company, select an investment banker or broker who has a demonstrated track record selling software companies.

174

Don't use an all-purpose broker to sell your company. You'll end up spending all your time trying to educate the broker on your business.

The second important factor is who you will be dealing with at the firm you are considering. Insist on dealing with a senior-level person *who knows your industry.* You don't want a "Junior Jock." Many of these firms hire bright, young, highly educated people who have no actual experience in industry. Although these are very nice, smart people, you can't afford to work with them. Insist on having your primary contact be a senior person with relevant experience and industry contacts.

The primary benefits of using a middleman, such as an investment banker or broker, are:

1. Identifying potential buyers
2. Contacting potential buyers
3. Getting an MNDA (mutual nondisclosure agreement) in place
4. Coaching you on next steps
5. Managing your expectations regarding valuation
6. Managing the acquisition process
7. Negotiating with a potential buyer

Selling a business is very emotional for the SFE. It helps to have a middleman between you and the buyer. This takes the emotion out of the negotiation. The SFE *always* thinks the business is more valuable than the eventual buyer, so it helps to have someone bring you back to reality.

Tips for your relationship with a middleman:

- You can negotiate the fees for this service. The fees are generally based on a percentage of the final selling price and usually range from 4 to 7 percent.

  They will want an upfront "retainer fee" to start the project. This number can be negotiated, as well as the "success fee."

  Also, most agreements call for a minimum payment (instead of the agreed-to percentage) regardless of the final selling price.

- Many brokers have a "proven process" for finding a buyer and selling a business. For example, most don't want you talking about selling price until you have gotten a potential buyer interested in your business.

  In my experience, this can be a huge waste of time. I found it is better to ask the potential buyer how they value businesses and what type of multiples they have paid in the past.

  It is also advisable for you to disclose the type of valuation metrics you are looking for. This saves everyone a lot of time.

You can present your expectations as a range. For example, you can say you expect to sell for two to three times annual revenue or five to eight times net income for the past twelve months.

This will get you on the same page upfront. If the potential buyer doesn't buy in to your valuation expectation, don't waste your time. Thank him for his time and move on.

- The best potential buyers are those who have done multiple acquisitions in the recent past. They know how to do this and aren't just out there kicking tires. Be wary of a potential acquirer where you would be their first.

The Language of M&A

These are some words, phrases, and acronyms that are commonly used during the selling process:

- *Balance sheet:* A financial report that summarizes a company's assets, liabilities, and shareholder's equity at a specific point in time. (Reported quarterly and at year-end.)
- *CAGR (compound annual growth rate):* The rate at which revenue (or profits) would have grown if they grew at a steady rate over a period of time.
- *Due diligence:* An audit that serves to confirm all material facts in regard to the sale.
- *Earn-out:* A contractual provision stating that the seller of the business is to get additional future compensation based on the business achieving certain future financial goals.
- *EBITDA (earnings before interest, taxes, depreciation, and amortization):* Used to analyze profitability.
- *Financial buyer:* A buyer who is primarily interested in a company's return on equity and cash flow.
- *GAAP (generally accepted accounting principles):* Principles, standards, and procedures used to compile financial statements.
- *Investment banker:* A person who helps an entrepreneur raise money, go public, or sell the company.
- *IPO (initial public offering):* The first sale of stock by a private company to the public.
- *Liquidity event:* An event that allows owners of a business to cash out some or all of their ownership shares.

- *LOI (letter of intent):* A nonbinding agreement that describes a buyer's intention to buy your company. Includes price, terms, assumptions, etc.
- *LTM (last twelve months):* Also known as TTM (trailing twelve months).
- *M&A (mergers and acquisitions):* A merger is a combination of two companies to form a new company, while an acquisition is the purchase of a company.
- *MNDA (mutual nondisclosure agreement):* A legal contract that signifies a confidential relationship between the parties involved.
- *Net income:* Total earnings or profits ("the bottom line").
- *Offering memorandum:* Provides potential buyers with information about your company.
- *Overlap:* Products or services that both buyer and seller have in common.
- *Recurring revenue:* That portion of revenue that is very likely to continue in the future. The revenue is predictable and stable and can be counted upon with a high degree of certainty.
- *ROI (return on investment):* Helps determine the effectiveness of any investment.
- *Roll-up:* When a number of similar companies merge to reduce costs.
- *Strategic partnership:* Code words used by a potential buyer that mean, "We want to buy you"—usually to round out their product portfolio.
- *Take a pass:* Words you don't want to hear from a potential buyer— "We're going to take a pass."
- *Valuation:* What someone thinks your company is worth.

Top Five Questions Asked by Potential Buyers

1. Why do you want to sell?
2. What keeps you up at night?
3. How many employees do you have by function or department?
4. What's your forecast for the next two years?
5. How long would you stay with the company after a transaction?

Many other questions relate to the income statement and the balance sheet (e.g. Why did this number increase/decrease? How does that number break down by percent? How much of your revenue is recurring revenue? What are your gross margins? What percent of revenue is EBIDA?).

Finding Potential Buyers

As previously mentioned, one benefit of forming partnerships with other companies is that they get to know you firsthand. These partners can be great potential acquirers.

It's good to have at least a couple of larger business partners who could view you as a potential strategic acquisition sometime in the future. You can get to know each other and mutually determine if a transaction makes sense.

The second good source of potential acquirers is companies in the same industry with complementary products or services.

The third good source is competitors. Some may be too small to acquire you, but a "merger of equals" may be possible. Multiple companies combining in the same industry is referred to as a roll-up.

The fourth good source is international companies who may want to expand into the United States. Their ability to expand is greatly enhanced by acquiring a US-based company with a good customer base and a proven product or service.

The fifth good source of potential acquirers is your customers.

The sixth good source is your suppliers.

Your investment banker or broker will contact companies in these categories using their contacts and database. They will send a two-page executive overview to these companies and follow up to see if there is interest in taking the next step.

The next step would be to have you and the potential buyer sign an MNDA (mutual nondisclosure agreement). A thirty- to sixty-minute telephone conversation then takes place to explore the opportunity, with all three parties on the call. Before the call, the broker sends a lengthy document to the potential buyer that includes information about your products or services, organization, finances, etc.

Just like a business plan, this document (sometimes called an offering memorandum) is overkill. Very few people actually read it.

I found that a ten-page (max) PowerPoint presentation was far more effective than the voluminous offering memorandum. An example might include the following:

Page	Description	Notes
1	Title Page	Include their logo and your logo
2	Positioning Statement	What makes you unique? (include value proposition)
3	Customers	Use logos
4	Products	Overview (keep it simple)
5	Services	Overview (keep it simple)
6	Milestones/History	Chapters
7	Last Three Years' Revenues/ Expenses/ Profits	
8	Forecasts	Next two years
9	Other Financial Information	Balance sheet, ownership breakdown, etc.
10	Next Steps	

Make sure to number each page so you can refer to a particular page while you're on the phone.

Even if the potential acquirer didn't spend much time preparing (this is the norm!), you can have a productive call using this ten-slide PowerPoint presentation.

Don't feel like you have to cover everything in your presentation. Just hit the highlights, and the potential acquirer can ask questions to fill in the blanks.

If there is mutual interest, you can go into more detail as a next step. This is actually a good way to gauge the interest of the buyer. This is a much more desirable scenario than swamping the buyer with data too early in the process. I found "more is less" when it comes to presentations.

After the Initial Conversation

It is very difficult to gauge the buyer's reaction to your pitch. It is impossible to forecast what may happen next. They have been trained not to appear overly enthusiastic about anything.

Usually the next step is to have a face-to-face meeting if the potential acquirer is interested in you.

The kiss of death is when the potential acquirer says, "You've got a nice little company here" after the conclusion of the conference call. What he really means is, "You're not worth my time," or he views you as a lifestyle business that is too small.

Another red flag appears if prospective buyers say they want to meet with you, but they want you to travel to them because they can't come to you. Any serious buyers will come to you for a meeting. If they won't, then they're just kicking the tires and are probably using you to compare to other potential acquisitions.

A meeting in itself doesn't mean a thing. I remember having a meeting with a CEO from one of GE's divisions. He came from across the country for the meeting and stayed for several hours. We really hit it off and had great synergy—it was a "1 + 1 = 3," as their saying goes.

I would have bet anything that they would make us an offer, but nothing ever happened. I guess he wanted us to be a business partner and resell his product.

The First of Six Near Misses

The first near miss was right in the middle of the Internet boom of the late 1990s. A $100 million (annual revenue) public company from the San Francisco area sent one of their scouts out to make contact with us at an industry trade show.

She invited us to visit them at their headquarters where we met the CEO, a guy named Larry Garlick (whom I admired greatly) and his management team. The meeting went well, and they promptly requested a follow-up meeting to begin the due-diligence process at our place in New Jersey.

I listened to a voice mail from Larry several weeks later. I was very excited to hear the following:

> *August 13, 1997 (9:13 p.m.)*
>
> *Hi Tim, this is Larry Garlick. I wanted to tell you what our next step is planned to be. I did get Corum's [our investment banker at the time] assessment of your valuation, and we've looked at that and have some folks assessing that.*
>
> *Also, we recently created an Employer Services Strategic Market Unit. The new general manager and our guy who heads up purchasing want (I believe) to come visit you, and I hope that would be consistent with where you want to go.*
>
> *I think something is negotiable here. I know we haven't talked much about Corum's results and the way we see things. I'm sure that there's*

a position that could be reached for us to partner more closely. So the GM is going to be giving you a call and trying to set something up. I sure hope we can accommodate that and move forward rapidly after that.

Okay. Thanks a lot. If you have any questions I'm at …. Thanks a lot.

The due-diligence meeting included six executives from their side. Their team included a guy who worked for the head of Product Development who was sent to try to understand how our product was built and how it worked.

The meeting went well and was very productive. Everyone was happy. Laurene and I were going to move to California and go to work for them for at least three years. We were very excited. We started working with a realtor on the West Coast that they used for all of their corporate relocations.

They had sent us a letter of intent (LOI) that indicated they were prepared to make us an offer at a very reasonable price. Things were progressing nicely, and it looked like a done deal.

And then a surprise … a major surprise. It came from the fellow who attended the due-diligence meeting who had just been promoted to the newly created position of general manager of the Employee Services Unit.

We had a brief discussion on the phone where he asked Laurene and me to fly to California to participate in a celebration to announce the acquisition. There was one problem with his request: we didn't have a signed agreement. When I explained that we didn't feel comfortable with the timing of the announcement without having an agreement covering the price, terms, and conditions of the sale, he freaked!

He said we weren't being cooperative, and the deal was off. He was like a little kid who took his ball and went home.

We were totally stunned, shocked, and angry. It was obvious that he didn't know what he was doing (in terms of an acquisition), and he was somehow threatened by me. He wouldn't even talk to me again after we talked on the phone.

I reached out to the CEO, Larry Garlick, and he said he was sorry but he was going to "stand by his [new] man."

Deal off. Game over. It was truly heartbreaking.

As a postscript, they developed their own eProcurement software and failed to make an impact on the market. Their product was taken off the market within two years. They lacked the "real world" expertise to make it successful.

To this day, I feel that if that acquisition had happened, we could have taken down the 800-pound gorilla in our market: Ariba.

> ## Take-Away #51
>
> Until the deal is done, anything can happen to derail it. Never stop running your company, even if you are sure a deal is right around the corner.

The Second Near Miss

The second near miss was with a $150 million, publicly traded payroll company also headquartered in Northern California. After several calls and a visit from the CEO, Laurene and I were invited to visit them in California. They rolled out the red carpet for us when we arrived. We met the entire management team and felt like it would be a good fit for us.

They did, too. There was absolutely no product overlap, and our target markets were identical. This was the scenario we had been hoping for. It was a strategic acquisition with a good valuation.

They sent two financial people to visit us for two days to conduct due diligence. We had dinner with them and everything seemed to be in order. They talked about "their model" for acquisition and gathered data to feed their model. This would help them finalize an offer to us. They returned to California with all the data needed to take the next step.

The CEO called me shortly thereafter and scheduled a meeting at our place to "finalize the deal." He said he would also have the senior VP of Marketing with him, and we could start planning press releases, new product plans, etc.

The day of the meeting arrived, and I walked with the CEO and his marketing guy into my office and closed the door. I was really excited!

We sat down, and after the obligatory corporate small talk, the CEO paused, took a deep breath, and said, "Tim, I can't buy your company." For a minute, I thought he was joking.

He went on to tell me that he had just bought an Internet-based human-resources software company for $70 million in order to get an Internet valuation for his stock.

He thought by buying the web-based HR company, he would increase his company's valuation to something north of ten times revenue.

Instead, his shareholders revolted. They thought the acquisition of the HR software company was a poor one, and that he had grossly overpaid for it.

He must have loved this company, because he paid thirty-five times revenue for it. They only had annual revenue of $2 million. They were actually smaller than we were!

Our meeting ended several minutes later. I honestly can't remember how it ended or what I said. I was in a state of shock.

The Third Near Miss

My newly hired senior VP of Marketing at PurchasingNet reached out to several companies to explore possible partnership opportunities. One company, a publicly traded computer-leasing company, said they wanted to visit us.

A week later, the CEO and the treasurer visited and said they were interested in acquiring us. We answered a few questions, and they left an hour later.

After a weeklong negotiation, we were invited to visit their headquarters in Virginia. The minute we walked into the lobby, we knew we didn't want anything to do with this company. Not only were their offices a filthy mess, but there were also girlie calendars hanging in employee cubicles. This was a complete cultural mismatch.

Out of courtesy, we spent a few hours with them, but we knew from the outset that this wasn't going to work for us. We later found out that they had offered several other companies a deal but were having trouble attracting a seller.

Take-Away #52

Visit your potential acquirer and evaluate their culture to make sure it is compatible with yours.

Near Miss Number Four

Two private investors backed by a midsize investment bank became interested in our company. The two investors had just sold their own company and received $30 million (each), and they were looking for something to do.

They wanted to buy all or part of our company using the investment bank's money. They wanted to assume the roles of CEO and COO, and they would operate remotely. Laurene and I would become their lieutenants.

Their plan was to raise the profile of PurchasingNet and position it for an IPO or big sale.

It sounded like a good plan, but it seemed to me that these two needed to put some skin in the game. What if their plan failed, and the company went down the tubes? Where would that leave us?

I decided to lay out a plan with milestones to achieve some specific objectives before we would transfer our shares in the company to them. The milestones included:

Find Strategic Investor	(Month 2)
Attract a Top-Tier Venture Capitalist	(Month 3)
Pay Existing Shareholders (us)	(Month 3)
Hire New Management Team	(Month 5)
Meet Current Sales Forecast	(Month 12)
IPO	(Month 15)

These were all the things they had verbally promised, but once they saw it in writing, they quickly backed away from the deal.

Take-Away #53

Whatever is promised, get it in writing. Trust your instincts if you smell a rat.

We had gone through a very comprehensive due-diligence process just prior to this. In retrospect, I'm glad they backed away from the deal. I don't believe they could have delivered on their promises, and September 11, 2001, was less than a year away. There was no way their plan could have been executed. We would have lost control of our company, and it probably would have gone under.

Near Miss Number Five

I probably received fifty cold calls a year from venture capitalists and private-equity firms wanting to invest in our company. I received one such call from a private-equity firm on the East Coast in 2008. I hit it off with their representative, and it resulted in a visit by two of their top executives.

These guys were trying to lowball me and were hoping we would sell for a song—a so-called "fire sale."

"We can be very patient," their CEO warned me, hoping I would cave in and accept their insulting offer.

Two times he visited me, and both times he promised get back to me within forty-eight hours with a letter of intent to buy the company.

From a product standpoint, this would have been a pretty good fit. Too bad I never hear from him again. I tried to follow up with him, but my calls were never returned.

Take-Away #54

When it comes to M&A, expect the unexpected. Once a potential acquirer loses interest, you'll never hear from them again.

Near Miss Number Six

This one was the most surprising and the most disappointing of all.

Our investment banker set up a meeting with a $5 billion (annual revenue) global software and services company.

They sent three people to the meeting. One was the general manager of a recently acquired company. We hit if off quite well. At one point during the meeting, we even exchanged high fives. The chemistry among us was excellent.

Afterward, I decided to call the CEO (who was not at the meeting), introduce myself, and get to know him. I called and arranged to meet him at Newark Airport. We had a nice lunch while he was waiting for a plane to the West Coast. The chemistry was excellent. We developed a good rapport very quickly.

About a month later, our teams got together at their office in New York City. This meeting was thought to be a time to confirm our understandings and get comfortable with each other before entering into an agreement.

The meeting was very productive. My team and I went out to a nice restaurant to celebrate. There would be no roadblocks to stop this deal.

About a week later, I was checking my voice mail and listened to a message from their director of Corporate Development: "Tim, we are going to take a pass on this deal. Thanks for your time, and good luck."

Two days later, I still couldn't believe it. I called the CEO, who told me the reason they passed was that he had been under the impression that we had three hundred enterprise customers (we actually had one hundred). There had been an internal communication problem. The CEO admitted that it was their communication problem and had not been misrepresented by me.

It was a shame. This one had all the elements in place—all the attributes of a great acquisition:

- CEO involvement
- Buyer had acquired many other companies
- Good cultural fit

- No product overlap
- Good valuation
- Good chemistry
- 1 + 1 = 3

Take-Away #55

In an acquisition, any one of a thousand elements or errors can trip you up. Expect the unexpected. Make sure to keep everyone on the same page, and have patience.

The Eventual Buyer

Each of the six near misses taught me something about the M&A process. Even though none of the deals had come to fruition, I now felt very comfortable and knowledgeable with each of the steps in the process.

We were in the middle of the Great Recession of 2008–2010 when the next M&A opportunity surfaced. I had read in a press release that our investment bank had just sold a software company to a hot, new Internet software company, Netsuite.

I called the general partner at the investment-banking firm to see what he thought about selling us to this company.

After a brief analysis, we concluded we would not be a good fit; there was too much product overlap. The investment banker suggested another possible buyer. I agreed to have a conversation to assess the possibilities of a deal.

The potential acquirer was based in Texas and was highly acquisitive. They were known for acquiring older software companies with significant revenue streams derived from maintenance and customer-support contracts. That fit our profile perfectly.

The buyer was also known for moving quickly if they became interested in a company.

They came to visit us on October 1, 2009. The meeting went well, and we had an LOI a week later.

The amount of the offer was considerably less than we hoped for, so we weren't particularly excited about it.

After a few weeks, we said we would seriously consider their offer if they would increase it and make sure our employees were treated fairly in the event of a layoff. We asked for more severance for our employees, especially those who had been with us for seven years or more.

The downside to being acquired by this company was that they had a history of laying off the majority of the employees and not pursuing new-name business. They would continue to service and support existing customers so they could keep the recurring revenue flowing. In fact, they would make every attempt to increase recurring revenue by "giving away" software modules that could increase value to the customer. In return, they would increase the annual maintenance bill. Enough customers bought into this model to make an acquisition extremely profitable.

We reached a verbal agreement on Thanksgiving weekend (deal making is a 24/7 endeavor).

We set a target for closing by December 31, 2009, to insure the lowest possible tax rate (at that time, President Obama was leaning toward increasing the Capital Gains Tax by 33 percent in 2010). That allowed four weeks to complete the entire due-diligence process. We were on our way!

Take-Away #56

Before you accept any offer, make sure your employees will be protected as much as possible.

STAGE 7:

Selling the Company

Money

Mind-Set	Marketing	Money	Management

Risk versus Reward Analysis

The SFE makes decisions by constantly analyzing risk versus reward. The question boils down to this: Does the risk of failing (losing money) outweigh the potential reward of doing something? This applies to any action, project, or strategy.

If there is high risk with very little potential reward, the decision will be to skip it. Conversely, if there is lots of upside with very little risk, the successful SFE will go for it every time.

This thought process is played out many times every day by SFEs, athletes, politicians, doctors, investors, etc. It helps apply logic to a confusing, complex, or emotional subject.

When the risk versus reward question is asked in the planning stage of a new business, the answer is that there is very little to lose and much to gain. Full speed ahead!

As the business progresses, the risks can become greater and the potential rewards smaller as more competitors enter the market and there is downward pressure on prices.

At a certain point, the risks outweigh the potential rewards, and it's time to get out. It's actually past time to get out by the time you've reached this conclusion.

As previously discussed, from a valuation standpoint, you would like to sell before you reach this point, but not everyone can.

Naturally, valuations are lower when the risks outweigh the rewards. Acquirers know this all too well.

We realized that we had reached this point, and the valuation was lower than it had been four years prior. There were considerations other than valuation, however. Personally, we were out of gas.

Deal Structure

We had been presented with several different deal structures over the years. The first was an "all stock" deal where the buyer gives you $X of their stock in exchange for all of your stock.

If an acquirer is publicly traded, you can gain liquidity by selling the shares. If the acquirer is privately owned, exchanging shares is swapping your risk for their risk. There is no chance of a liquidity event in the short term. I never wanted to swap my risk for their risk. At least I could manage my risk.

The best valuations are usually in all-stock deals. However, you may not be able to sell your shares immediately on the open market, so it is best to implement a hedging strategy to lock in your gains. A certified financial planner can help you figure out how to do this.

On the other side of the spectrum are all-cash deals. Valuations are lower, but remember, cash is king! This type of deal typically contains an "earn-out." This is a provision that allows the buyer to withhold part of the purchase price and pay it only after you have met certain objectives. These can be revenue or profitability goals.

Earn-outs are unfair and should be avoided. The reason I say this is because you will be working for someone who can change priorities and require you to focus on different tasks that can easily distract you from achieving your goals. Jack Welch, former CEO of General Electric, agrees that earn-outs are counterproductive for everyone (*Businessweek,* July 20, 2007).

Our Deal

If you look at our M&A transaction, I would say the price was less than we wanted (I think this is probably true for most sellers), but the terms were very favorable for us.

The terms of the deal included 100 percent cash paid at closing, minimal escrow (less than 10 percent of the total), no earn-out, and fast transition (two-month consulting agreement for Laurene and me).

Due Diligence

I was surprised how much information was required to complete the sale. Our controller, Eileen Durkin (also our daughter-in-law, with an MBA from Fordham University), and Laurene worked nonstop for about three weeks to provide all the material needed by the buyer.

The information requested included customer contracts, HR records, employee agreements, payroll information, organization charts, past two years of income statements and balance sheets, and our employee handbook.

Fortunately, we had implemented automated systems like CRM (customer-relationship management) and our own software to manage A/R, A/P, etc. These systems allowed us to access the data required for a fast close. We had also managed our company and employee records carefully over the years, so we were able to produce past employee agreements as well. It was important to the buyer that we could produce documentation that all developers acknowledged that ownership of the computer code and all inventions belonged to the company. I doubt this would have stopped the deal, but it was one less thing they could use to lower the price.

Take-Away #57

Keep good records on past and current employees and customers. It is essential for an eventual acquisition.

As we counted down to our December 31, 2009, closing, we received a very surprising letter from a large law firm representing one of our customers. The letter stated that they had a patent on a couple of eProcurement software applications and wanted us to license this software *from them*. This is typically a veiled threat that "we will sue you if you don't pay up." Where I'm from, they call this extortion.

The applications that were patented by our customer looked like the software they had licensed from us ten years prior! At first we thought this might spook our buyer, but they hung in there with us and just increased the escrow they withheld from us to cover half the potential litigation costs. (Note: There never was litigation, and we received the escrow one year later.)

Valuation Methods

In the final analysis, valuation models that you read about aren't really that important, especially when it's a buyer market. The valuation metrics used by the buyer are crucial to the ultimate purchase price. Your desires are secondary.

Our buyer used a multiple of recurring annual revenue based on the last twelve months. The multiple was lower than those seen during the Internet boom. There's no question that we sold four to five years after the valuation peak. The global financial crisis certainly took the air out of the M&A balloon in 2009.

Coming Down the Home Stretch

Selling your company is a very stressful situation. You're on the edge of your seat and very excited as you get closer to executing the transaction.

We ran into several potential snags at the eleventh hour. First, an old line of credit that we had paid off several years before showed as still being open, and the guy at the bank who had the responsibility to properly terminate the line of credit was on vacation until after the first of the year. We overcame this minor obstacle, but it added a little more stress to an already stressful situation.

Then it was discovered that a New Jersey company that was legitimately using our old company name (American Tech, Inc.) had failed to pay taxes, and the state had placed a tax lien on their business. It appeared to our buyer's law firm that *we* had a tax lien on our business. This, of course, was not the case, but it caused lots of excitement. Our law firm clarified the situation for the buyer, and we eventually moved forward.

We had about six or seven rapid-fire incidents just like this. It felt like playing the carnival game Whack-a-Mole—once one issue was clobbered, another one surfaced.

STAGE 7:

Selling the Company

Management

N o matter what you think might happen regarding the sale of your business, keep running the business as you normally would. It's okay to cut back on longer-term investments for a month while the M&A cycle is coming to a conclusion, but continue day-to-day operations in a normal fashion.

Keep Quiet!

You may need other team members to get involved in the process of selling the business. I tried to keep most employees out of the process. It's not that I wanted to withhold needed information, but I was very aware that: a) the deal might not happen, and b) people stop working and spend their time in the gossip mill trying to figure out what they're going to do after the sale, who the new owners will keep, and so on.

It's better to wait until the deal closes and then announce it. In our case, we were asked to continue to operate the company for several weeks after closing until the new management team could be assembled in the United States for the transition meetings.

Once the acquirer was ready for the transition, I gathered the employees to tell them about the acquisition. The following are excerpts from my meeting notes with the employees on January 12, 2010:

On December 31, 2009, there was a change of ownership of PurchasingNet, Inc.

Laurene and I will remain with the company as consultants, but there will be a new management team. You will meet them tomorrow at 10:00 a.m.

Personally, Laurene and I have mixed emotions about this transaction. On one hand, we've been doing this for twenty-eight years, and it's time to move to the next phase of our lives.

2004 through 2007 were great years for PNet. 2008 and 2009 were very difficult years for all of us.

The truly good news is that PNet now has a large global company behind it.

I would characterize the new PNet management team as very smart and very accomplished. They were educated at institutions like Stanford, Harvard, Dartmouth, and Rice, and have significant experience running software companies.

In short, the PNet product and company will now have what it needs to thrive and grow.

Of course, there will be changes. For many of you, these will be welcome changes and will lead to more professional growth and opportunity. Some of you may seek opportunities outside of the company.

As I mentioned previously, the new management team will be meeting with you tomorrow at 10:00 a.m. to outline their vision for the future. They will let you know where you stand in the new organization as quickly as possible. They will answer your questions starting tomorrow. There will be five people visiting tomorrow. Each functional area will be covered.

Laurene and I will try to talk to you individually over the next several days.

Thank you for your hard work and sacrifice. It's been a long ride and a good ride.

Everyone except those at a customer site should plan on being here before 10:00 a.m. tomorrow.

Please do not tell customers, partners, suppliers, former employees, etc. That will all be handled by the new management team.

Of course, you are free to share this with your families.

And so you are probably asking yourself, "What does this mean to me?" At this point, we don't know (and they don't know) the specific plan. This will be formulated starting tomorrow."

After twenty-eight years, this was like an out-of-body experience. Most people were shocked to hear the news. Many of them had questions that we just couldn't answer at that moment in time.

Creating a "Soft Landing" for Employees

When you think about how you arrived at this point, most SFEs would say that it couldn't have happened without their employees and management team.

In many cases, it is important to the acquirer that you have selected and developed your team to carry on in your absence.

It is important to provide as much severance as possible for those who will not be staying with the new company. We negotiated an enhanced severance plan for longtime employees. Employees also received a payment from our loyalty-incentive program if they were eligible. We felt that with the combination of transition time, severance, loyalty-incentive payment, and unemployment insurance, most employees would be okay. Others would remain with the company.

Closing

We won our race against time. Closing was concluded two hours before the close of business on December 31, 2009.

A sample letter of intent and due-diligence checklist are included in Appendix A and B.

Our journey was now complete!

My Top Ten Mulligans

As all golfers know, a mulligan is a do-over when you hit a less-than-satisfactory shot. These are ten mulligans I wish I had taken.

Mulligan #1	Spent more time networking with potential acquirers. Could have resulted in a faster sale at a higher valuation.
Mulligan #2	Hired better managers. Ultimately, we "hit the wall" and had difficulty growing beyond forty employees. We gave it our all, but we could have used more talented and experienced managers.
Mulligan #3	Established a board of advisors. Could have taken some pressure off me and provided some outside ideas and insights.
Mulligan #4	Spun off a new company at the height of the Internet hype era. This company could have concentrated on web-based applications and IPOed, resulting in increased company value.
Mulligan #5	Done more due diligence on our Asian partner. Could have saved us a bundle.
Mulligan #6	Picked a better name for our company. When we introduced payables and invoice software, the name PurchasingNet just didn't hack it.
Mulligan #7	Concentrated on SEO before committing to paid search. Could have saved us a small fortune.
Mulligan #8	Made it easier to do business with us. Our pricing model became too complicated for people to understand. It resulted in lost business.
Mulligan #9	Figured out a better way to qualify prospects. We wasted an awful lot of time and money "chasing rabbits."
Mulligan #10	Utilized a more mainstream technology platform. Would have exposed us to more potential acquirers.

That said, we did an awful lot right. But a good entrepreneur learns from his or her mistakes. That's part of any good management system—feedback, measurement, analysis, and corrective action.

Hopefully, you can take what I learned and increase your probability of success.

Postscript

Prescription for Economic Recovery

The vast majority of new jobs are created by entrepreneurial companies. It only makes sense to create a positive environment for all entrepreneurs so new jobs can be created and the economy can grow. Some of the things that can be done by government to create this climate include:

Reduce tax rates and provide tax incentives (such as R&D credits). Remember the "SFE reflex action"? Every cost increase is met with an equal and opposite cost reduction. It works in reverse too. Reducing taxes encourages hiring.

Reduce government regulation. This could include actions like eliminating patents on software, healthcare restrictions, tax simplification, etc. This would reduce the entrepreneur's costs and lead to more hiring.

Make other creative policy changes. Lowering the Medicare age to 55 would reduce healthcare costs for the entrepreneur while encouraging SFEs to hire people over the age of 55. This would also help the "Boomer Generation" (78 million people in the United States) who will be retiring over the coming decade. This demographic group will create a huge economic crisis as fewer than 20 percent of Boomers have pension plans (other than Social Security).

Generate additional tax revenue. Remember the SFE Sink Analogy? There are only two ways to increase the level of water. One is to increase the flow of water from the faucet. In this case, increasing the flow means increasing taxes. Here are some areas for consideration:

- Legalize and tax online poker and other games.
- Legalize and tax all sports gambling.
- Perform means testing on Social Security and Medicare.
- Legalize and tax medical marijuana. Establish controls similar to those used for alcoholic beverages. Harvard economist Jeffrey Miron calculates this could generate $8.7 billion in tax revenues and similar savings in law enforcement costs.
- Tax property and land owned by religious groups.
- Tax high-frequency stock trading.

Reduce government spending. The second way to increase the level of water in the sink is to prevent water from going down the drain. This means reducing outflow (spending). Here are some programs that should be eliminated:

- Department of Commerce—In my thirty-year SFE career, I never once had this organization contact me or make me aware of any value they could add to my businesses. Other departments could also be eliminated, such as Energy, Education, and Agriculture.
- Census Bureau—This could be outsourced to private companies, such as Visa, MasterCard, ADP, or Facebook (not kidding!).
- National Public Radio—There is no need for this program. The private sector has ample choice for radio channels.
- Entitlement Programs—These need to be reduced even if it is not politically popular. I would recommend starting with means testing for Social Security and Medicare.

Develop a national energy policy. In the 1970s, '80s, and '90s, we lost a large percentage of our manufacturing jobs to other countries. Most of them will never come back. The housing and financial-services markets were the growth engine of the late 1990s and early 2000s. These two industries suffered tremendously in the Great Recession of 2008–2010. It only makes sense to develop a national energy policy that helps create new jobs and enables energy independence for the United States. This would also help restore our national pride. We would have a common purpose and ultimately improve our national security while jump-starting our economy.

Improve entrepreneurial education. We need to create more good entrepreneurs faster. We also don't want half of all new businesses to fail within five years. We need to create more new businesses and improve the success rate. Can education help achieve these goals? I say yes. I believe at least 60 percent of the SFE's success is ultimately determined by knowledge and skills that are teachable. The other 40 percent is determined by intelligence, common sense, leadership abilities, and timing. For the most part, you either have these or you don't. No amount of education can improve these factors. That said, if we can improve the knowledge and skills component through education and training, we can improve the overall success rate of the entrepreneur. This will bolster the economy and create many new jobs.

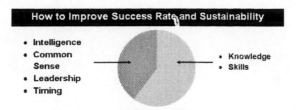

How to Improve Success Rate and Sustainability

- Intelligence
- Common Sense
- Leadership
- Timing

- Knowledge
- Skills

Unlocking entrepreneurial potential is the surest path to prosperity.

About the Author

Tim McEneny cofounded PurchasingNet, Inc., in 1982. Despite competing with three large, publicly owned, global companies, he successfully navigated his self-funded software company through all seven stages of the business cycle, including a sale of the company in 2009. The company survived and thrived despite five recessions and four disruptive technology changes during its twenty-eight-year history.

An award-winning innovator, McEneny developed the first Windows-based and first web-based automated purchasing software packages. He was named a "Pro-to-Know" four times by *Supply Chain Executive Magazine*.

Starting from scratch, his start-up created software that was purchased by 1,400 midsize to large companies to improve productivity. This was achieved in a highly competitive, dynamic market without third-party equity investors.

McEneny is a successful self-funded entrepreneur. His mentoring and insights can help you achieve the American dream, however you may define it.

TimMcEneny@TimMcEneny.com

APPENDIX A

Sample Letter of Intent

Gentlemen:

We are pleased to submit this letter of intent, which sets forth the terms and conditions pursuant to which the Acquiring Company would proceed with the transaction described below with the SFE Company.

1. **Transaction Structure:** Acquiring Company anticipates that it would acquire 100 percent of the capital stock of SFE Company free and clear of any options, liens, or other claims, including the settlement of all in-the-money options. This transaction would be structured as a merger. Acquiring Company will make a 338(h)(10) election and SFE Company will be required to make a similar election upon closing.

2. **Acquisition Considerations:** Acquiring Company is prepared to offer a purchase price of $X in cash, paid at closing.

3. **Retention Agreements:** Acquiring Company will contract with Employee A, Employee B, and Employee C for a period of ninety (90) days following the acquisition. The contract rate will be $X for each per month for a total of $X each for the ninety days. Any future contract work between these employees will be mutually negotiated at a future date.

4. **Employee Severance:** For all employees that are involuntarily exited, Acquiring Company will pay five weeks of severance for employees with less than seven years' tenure and twelve weeks for employees with greater than seven years' tenure.

5. **Bank Debt Settlement:** SFE Company must have positive cash bank balances at the close of June 30th with no outstanding debt obligations or lines of credit.

6. **Transaction Fees:** Transaction fees, including broker and legal fees, will be paid by the respective party incurring the transaction expenses. SFE Company transaction fees will be paid by SFE Company owners.

7. **Escrow/Indemnifications:** Provided due diligence is completed as expected, no indemnification, escrow, or other liability post-close will be required.

8. **Financing:** The purchase price will be funded from cash currently available to Acquiring Company and is not subject to any financing contingency.

9. **Due Diligence:** Closing of a transaction is subject to further customary due diligence. Acquiring Company will be allowed further access to the books, records, products, customers, and management of SFE Company. Reference calls will be conducted with key customers when appropriate. Of particular importance during diligence will be an updated review of recurring revenue and retention rates.

10. **Contingencies:** Acquiring Company currently anticipates that the closing of a transaction would be contingent upon the following:
    a. Acquiring Company shall have conducted its due diligence investigation and be satisfied with the findings thereof.
    b. Any transaction would be subject to the negotiation and execution of definitive agreements with mutually agreeable terms. The agreement would contain representations, warranties, covenants and conditions customary in similar transactions, including the obtaining of all necessary third party consents.
    c. There shall be no material adverse change in the assets, business or financial condition of SFE Company prior to the closing.

11. **Corporate Authorization:** Final agreement is subject to approval by Acquiring Company's Board of Directors.

12. **Timetable:** We endeavor to close and fund the transaction on June 30th of the current year.

13. **Exclusivity:** For a thirty (30) day period commencing upon acceptance of this proposal, SFE Company will negotiate exclusively with Acquiring Company and will refrain from negotiating or entering into an agreement with other parties that contemplate the sale of capital stock or assets of SFE Company.

14. **Timing:** This proposal is effective until MM/DD/YYYY, at 5:00 p.m. EST.

This proposal is nonbinding and subject to further discussions with you to address the terms of any agreement we may ultimately reach. This letter is not a commitment to enter into a definitive final agreement. We look forward to your response.

Sincerely yours,
Acquiring Company   SFE Company
By: _____   By: _____
Name: Name:
Title: Title:

Appendix B

Sample Due-Diligence Checklist

1. **Basic Corporate Documents (for corporation and all subsidiaries)**
   a. Certificate of incorporation, including all amendments
   b. Bylaws, including all amendments
   c. Minutes of all meetings and written consent of directors and shareholders for the past two years
   d. List of all states and countries where property is owned or leased or where employees are located, and a brief statement of the nature of business conducted in each location
   e. List of all subsidiaries describing nature of ownership

2. **Shareholder Information**
   a. Shareholder list as of a recent date
   b. List of outstanding options and warrants, including date of grant, exercise prices, number of shares subject to option, names and addresses of option holders
   c. Contracts of plans concerning outstanding or proposed stock options, warrants, or rights
   d. All material press releases issued by the company in the past five years

3. **Securities Issuances**
   a. Samples of common and preferred stock certificates, warrants, options, debentures, and any other outstanding securities
   b. Any agreement relating to sales of securities by the company

    c.   All voting trust, shareholder, or other similar agreements covering any of the company's shares

4. **Corporate Finance**
   a. Bank line of credit agreements, including any amendments, renewal letters, notices, waivers, etc.
   b. Other documents and agreements evidencing borrowing, whether secured or unsecured by the company, including loan and credit agreements, promissory notes, and other evidences of indebtedness, and all guarantees
   c. All documents and arrangements evidencing other material financing arrangements, including sale and leaseback arrangements, installment purchases, etc.
   d. Correspondence with lenders, including all compliance reports submitted by the company or its independent public accounts for the past three years

5. **Financial Information (for three most recent fiscal years)**
   a. Financial or operation plans or projections
   b. Management letters or special reports by auditors and any response thereto
   c. Audited financial statements, including historical quarterly financial statements
   d. Material (including financial projections), if available, distributed to members of board of directors and committees thereof in connection with recent meetings
   e. Description of any change in accounting methods of principles
   f. Aging schedules for accounts receivable and accounts payable

6. **Operations**
   a. List of major suppliers showing total and type of purchases from each supplier during the last and current fiscal years
   b. Material contracts in ordinary course of business (e.g. contracts within the last three years accounting for a large part of the company's purchases or sales)
   c. Contracts not in ordinary course of business (e.g. contracts within the last three years relating to joint ventures, partnerships, resellers, acquisitions, or depositions)
   d. Form of product warranties of the company

 e. List of all third-party products/software included in company's products and/or offerings (provide associated licenses or proof product is licensed as freeware)

 f. Description of any toxic chemicals used in production and manner of storage and disposition, and description of any EPA or other investigation or claim

7. **Products and Competition**

 a. List of any trademarks, trade names, brands, copyrights, or service marks

 b. Permits for conduct of business, including licenses, franchises, concessions and distributorship agreements, and conditional sales contracts

 c. List of principal products in each line of business with short description of products

 d. List of principal competitors by product

 e. List of all foreign and domestic patents and patent licenses held by the company and of patent applications

8. **Sales and Marketing**

 a. List of the company's largest customers, including revenue derived from each and products/services purchased by each during the past two years

 b. Consultant's, engineer's, or management reports and marketing studies related to broad aspects of the business, operations, or products of the company

 c. Samples of marketing and sales literatures used for various products

9. **Employees**

 a. Number of employees broken down by division and department, and a management organization chart

 b. Forms of employment agreements and employee confidentiality agreements

 c. Employee benefit, pension, profit-sharing, compensation, and other plans

 d. Collective bargaining agreements or other material labor contracts

 e. Description of commissions paid to managers, agents, or other employees.

 f. Description of any significant labor problems or union

activities the company has experienced, including any collective bargaining agreements

10. **Officers and Directors**
   a. Management employment agreements, if any
   b. Schedule of all compensation paid in past three years to officers, directors, and key employees, showing separately salary, bonuses, and noncash compensation (e.g., use of cars, property, etc.)
   c. Bonus plans, retirement plans, pension plans, deferred compensation plans, profit sharing, and management incentive agreements
   d. Agreements for loans to and any other agreements (including consulting and employment contracts) with officers or directors
   e. Description of any transactions between the company and any "insider" (i.e., any officer, director, or owner of a substantial amount of the company's securities) or any associate of an "insider," or between or involving any two or more such "insiders"

11. **Tangible Property**
   a. List of material real and personal property owned by the company
   b. Documents of title, mortgages, deeds of trust, leases, and security agreements pertaining to the properties listed in *a* above

12. **Litigation and Audits**
   a. All letters from counsel sent to auditors for year-end and current interim audits (i.e. "litigation letters")
   b. Pleadings and other material documents regarding any material litigation, arbitration or investigation to which the company is a party or in which it may become involved
   c. Information regarding consent decrees, judgments, etc., under which the company has continuing of contingent obligations

13. **Insurance**
   a. Schedule of copies of all material insurance policies of the company, covering property, liabilities, and operations (e.g.

Errors & Omissions Insurance, Workers' Compensation, state disability plans for each state where employees are located, Commercial Crime Coverage, etc.)

b. Schedule of any other insurance policies in force, such as "key man" policies, director indemnification policies, errors and omission, or product liabilities policies.

14. Government Regulations and Filings

a. Summary of all OSHA inquiries (if any)

b. Summary of all EPA, EEO, etc., inquiries (if any)

c. Status of contracts subject to Renegotiation Act

d. List of how the company's products are classified for import/export

e. Summary of what export process is in place at company

f. Copy of foreign, US, state, and local income-tax returns for last three fiscal years and their status (i.e., Have all returns been filed? All taxes been paid? Any audits by taxing authorities?)

g. Status of compliance with foreign, US, and state regulations (e.g. environmental protection, price controls, product allocations)

Resources

www.constantcontact.com	Constant Contact
www.godaddy.com	Go Daddy
www.directincorporation.com	Direct Incorporation
www.sbresources.com	Small Business Resources
www.webex.com	Cisco WebEx
www.gotomeeting.com	GoToMeeting
www.sales-sense.com	Sales Sense
www.investopedia.com	Investopedia
www.facebook.com	Facebook
www.twitter.com	Twitter
www.skype.com	Skype
www.google.com	Google
www.yahoo.com	Yahoo!
www.webbreez.com	Webbreez

REFERENCES

Bosma, Niels, and Jonathan Levie. 2009. "Executive Report." *Global Entrepreneurship Monitor.*

Fleischner, Michael H., and Greg Wuttke. *SEO Made Simple: Strategies for Dominating the World's Largest Search Engine, Second Edition.* La Vergne, TN: Lightning Source.

Kaplan, Philip J. 2002. *F'd Companies: Spectacular Dot-Com Flameouts,* New York: Simon & Schuster.

Levinson, Jay Conrad, with Jeannie Levinson and Amy Levinson. *Guerilla Marketing, Fourth Edition.* New York: Houghton Mifflin.

Naisbitt, John. 1988. *Megatrends: Ten New Directions Transforming Our Lives.* New York: Warner Books.

Spors, Kelly K. 2008. *The 100-Page Start-up Plan—Don't Bother,* The Wall Street Journal Sunday. February 17, 2008. Scripps Treasure Coast Newspapers.

Strunk, William, and E. B. White. 2008. *The Elements of Style, 50th Anniversary Edition.* New York: Longman.

Stull, Craig with Phil Myers and David Meerman Scott. 2007. *The Secrets of Market-Driven Leaders.* Scottsdale, Arizona: Pragmatic Marketing.

Townsend, Robert C. 2007. *Up the Organization: How to Stop the Corporation from Stifling People and Strangling Profits, Commemorative Edition.* Hoboken, NJ: Jossey-Bass.

Welch, Jack, and Suzy Welch. 2007. *The Reverse Hostage Syndrome.* Ideas— The Welch Way. July 30, 2007. Bloomberg Businessweek.

Welch, Jack, with John Byrne. 2001. *Jack: Straight from the Gut.* New York: Warner Books.